THE OCCULT ...
HERBS ...

Reveals the fascinating part played by herbs in alchemy, astrology, healing, magic and religion. Includes notes on fruit ceremonies, the cult of Bacchus, vegetable drugs, love philtres, herbs of the planets and plants of the Zodiac.

THE OCCULT PROPERTIES OF HERBS AND PLANTS

by

W.B. CROW
D.Sc., Ph.D.

THE AQUARIAN PRESS
Wellingborough, Northamptonshire

First published 1969
Fifth Impression 1976
Second Edition, revised, enlarged and reset, 1980

ISBN 0 85030 196 3 (UK)
ISBN 0 87728 456 3 (USA)

Photoset by
Specialised Offset Services Limited, Liverpool
and printed in Great Britain by
Weatherby Woolnough Ltd., Wellingborough
Northants, England

CONTENTS

NOTE

We advise our readers that they should not use any of the healing plants mentioned, except under the guidance of a skilled practitioner. Even plants commonly used for healing may be very dangerous in the wrong doses, or if the wrong part of the plant is taken.

CHAPTER ONE

THE NATURE OF HERBS

If we consider plants as they actually are, and not because of their use or medical properties, we can class them roughly as herbs, shrubs and trees, with some intermediate stages, such as undershrubs.

Herbs have no woody stems above ground. They die down in winter, and pass the cold season either as a persistent underground stem, which may be woody, or the individual plant dies altogether, and only seeds remain to reproduce the plant. Sometimes the underground persistent part is a stem with non-green scale leaves, with various shapes to which such names as rhizome, tuber, corm, bulb are applied, and to which roots or rootlets[1] are attached.

The shape of the overground shoot varies very much according to whether the leaves are crowded together on the stem or whether they are more widely separated.

A Common Plan

In spite of the immense diversity among the thousands of known plant species there is a certain common plan of structure observable throughout a large part of the vegetable kingdom. Hippocrates (460-377 B.C.), that great physician of antiquity, recognized the plant as a compound individual, *i.e.* a unit made of many smaller units. Each unit was a

---

[1] A rootlet is simply a small root.

shoot, *i.e.* a stem with leaves. Only a few of the shoots or a single one at the base may have a root or roots attached.

In more recent times, but before the rise of Darwinism, that great initiate of the arcane sciences, Goethe (1749-1832), taught the doctrine of the *Urpflanze*, the primitive plant, that living form or pattern which exists as an arcane archetype in all the higher plants. It is not an ancestral species, in the sense of evolution, but a reality expressing kinship, and therefore implying genetic relationship, hence possible descent from a common ancestor.

In 1790, in his *Metamorphosis of Plants*, Goethe showed how the vegetative or non-reproductive shoot in the higher plants is succeeded by the flower or reproductive shoot, equivalent or homologous to the preceding, a principle accepted in scientific botany at the present day.

But it was known, even to the ancients, that some plants, such as seaweeds and fungi, do not conform to this pattern. They possess neither stems, leaves or roots, still less the equivalents in the flower. Seaweeds, it is true, have leaf-like lobes and stalks, but careful examination shows they are not arranged as in flowering plants, with the leaves arising from *nodes*, sometimes separated by leafless lengths of stem called *internodes*. The fungus body, in fact, is a mere tangle of cellular threads and the fructification of a fungus is in no way the equivalent of a flower.

Kinds of Plants

We must now outline the great groups of plants, so that the reader who is not well up in botany may know the sort of plants we are referring to in the later parts of this book.

First of all there is a great section of the vegetable kingdom in which the three main organs of the non-reproductive parts (root, leaf and stem), not to mention the reproductive flower, are missing. Instead, they all have an undifferentiated plant body, called the *thallus*. Of this great section there are three main kinds: algae, fungi and lichens.

Algae

The algae include the seaweeds, the pond-scums of freshwater and vast numbers of microscope organisms forming a great part of the free-floating population (plankton) of the sea. The last named (and many of the pond-scums) are apparently made up each of a single cell.

Many of the pond-scums are nothing more than rows of cells (filaments) sometimes much branched. On the sea-shore we find the green sheet of cells called the sea-lettuce, but most seaweeds are brown (wracks or kelps) or red (dulses) and some of the brown are of gigantic size. Seaweeds only live in relatively shallow water around the shore, as they require light for photosynthesis.

Some algae have sexual reproduction, often also spores which float or swim in the water; they also reproduce vegetatively by the simple expedient of breaking off pieces. All their reproductive organs are very small.

Fungi

Fungi, unlike the algae, largely live on land. Many are parasites on land plants, others live on decaying matters in the soil. Consequently they have no green pigment (*chlorophyll*) and do not need the light.

Mushrooms may be grown in damp cellars. The non-reproductive part of a fungus is merely a mass of fine much-branded filaments (*mycelium*) as in mushroom spawn, but the reproductive organs are often of large size. What we call the mushroom itself is the reproductive organs (*fructification*) producing millions of fine spores.

Lichens

Lichens are really double organisms, living on land. Their reproductive organs are like small editions of those of the fungi. They belong to fungi, in fact, but the rest of the fungus is not a mass of fine branched filaments but a flat or lobed thallus like a seaweed.

This is because the lichen has taken into partnership a number of small algae, and these help is to synthesize the food, with the aid of the light. Hence the almost leaf-like form of the lichen body.

Mosses are small leafy plants, with stems but no roots. Sex organs are formed on mosses and the embryo produced grows, not into another moss, but a spore-producing structure, which remains attached to the moss plant. The spores reproduce new moss plants. Liverworts are like mosses, but are often creeping and some have lobes instead of separate leaves.

Ferns

When we come to the ferns we reach the full development of the vegetative parts, for there are roots, stems and leaves. In the tropics some ferns reach the stature of trees. Most ferns have

enormous divided leaves. On these spores are
produced.

The spores do not grow into new fern plants, but
into a tiny green leaf-life object called the *prothallus*.
This has the sex-organs on it which produce the
embryo that grows into the fern-plant.

A similar life-history is seen in the club-mosses,
which resemble overgrown mosses, but are quite
unrelated, and in the horsetails, strange to say, as
the latter two kinds only have the smallest of leaves.

Cone-bearing Plants

We now come to the cone-bearing plants, which
include some of the largest trees. The cone is the
reproductive part. There are two kinds of cone, one
the male the other the female. They both really
produce spores, but the female spore germinates
inside the ovule which produces the seed, after it
has been fertilized by the pollen tube which is
produced by the pollen of the male cone.

There are two kinds of cone plants, one with big
compound leaves like the fern. This type includes
the cycads. The other kind has small leaves adapted
to colder climes. This includes the larches, pines,
firs and yews, adapted to colder regions, where they
form forests. The cycads, on the other hand live in
the tropics.

Flowering Plants

Let us now consider the flowering plants. The
flower differs from a cone, in that the ovules, which
are going to form seeds, are enclosed in a structure
called an *ovary*. As in the cone plants, spores are
produced, the female in the ovule forming an

embryo-sac making the egg and the male forming
the pollen tube containing the male cell for
fertilizing the egg.

The flowering plants are an enormous group with
a wide range of form and growing in very diverse
environments. There are two groups:
monocotyledons, technically distinguished by
having a single seed-leaf or cotyledon, and
Dicotyledons, having two. If they grow into trees
their internal structure is quite different in the
trunk.

Monocotyledons have leaves with parallel veins
and no stalks, with few exceptions, the parts of the
flower are usually in twos or threes, there is no
distinction between petals and sepals.

Dicotyledons have net-veined leaves, often with
stalks, the parts of the flower tending to be arranged
in fours or fives and sepals are generally small and
green, thus contrasting with the often brightly
coloured petals.

Grasses are Monocotyledons with inconspicuous
flowers, and sedges are closely related.

Lilies and their kin, such as crocus, autumn
crocus, onion, hyacinth, tulip, yam, narcissus, iris,
ginger and the orchids, generally have conspicuous
flowers and large bulbous underground parts.
Palms and aroids have numerous small flowers,
often accompanied by an enormous leaf called a
spathe. The so-called arum lily is a beautiful
example. All these are Monocotyledons.

Dicotyledons are even more numerous.

They include catkin-trees, with inconspicuous
flowers, such as willows and poplars, bog-myrtle,
walnuts, birch, alder, hazel, hornbeam, beech,

sweet chestnut, oak, elm, and some herbs such as stinging nettles and the goosefoot and chickweed family.

Another section of Dicotyledons includes flowers with conspicuous separate petals, as in buttercups, poppies, cresses, the rose family, the pea family, the geranium and holly groups, the buckthorns, vines, mallows, violets, myrtles, parsley group, and many more.

Finally, a section with showy flowers having united petals includes the heaths, primroses, thrifts, gentians, olive, ash, lilac, dead-nettle family, potato family, foxglove family, madders, gourd family and the sunflower and daisy group in which many tiny flowers (*florets*) form a single flower-head.

CHAPTER TWO

HERBS AS FOODS

Sympathetic magic depends on the belief that what happens to anything is to some extent dependent upon what happens to something else with which a magical link has been forged.

Today we take food for granted. Food is just food, and that is all. A few people, perhaps, will have the decency to thank God for it, but to primitive man spiritual forces, often personified, were hidden behind foods, both animals and vegetable.

The Seven Cereals

Nowhere else are these more obvious than in the seven chief cereals which formed the food of man from the Neolithic age, when the practice of agriculture began. What was done then was magic, designed to utilize such occult forces, in order to ensure the growth of crops and to stave off famine from the community.

These magical practices persisted into later times in human history, and were incorporated into religion, as shown by Sir James Frazer in his monumental *The Golden Bough*. The corn-spirit was personified in various ways, by a human being or even an animal. The same was sacrificed, or apparently sacrificed and came to life again, symbolizing the renewal of the crops.

The cereals are members of the grass family, which differ from the wild species in yielding large and abundant grain.

Wheat is the cereal of Britain, the Mediterranean region and Western Asia. Wheat in the ceremonies was symbolized by the wheat-mother, the wheat-bride, the wheat-man, or by a dog, wolf, goat, cow or sow.

Rye is mainly the cereal of Germany and Russia, both famous for rye-bread. It was symbolized by the rye-mother, an old woman or a dog, wolf, goat or sow.

Oats are cultivated in more northerly parts of Europe. Hence porridge is the national dish of Scotland. It was symbolized by the oats-mother, the oats-bride, also by a stallion, a cow, a goat, a sow or a wolf.

Maize was originally cultivated only in America, where the natives had a maize-mother, or goddess of the maize.

Rice is cultivated in the damp tropics, being the staple food of the South of Asia, where there were ceremonies of the rice bride and bridegroom, and of the rice mother and rice child.

Millet of various kinds is cultivated in Italy, Germany and many dry parts of Asia. Among the Ainu of the North of Japan there is worshipped the god of millet.

Their Mysterious Origin

As we have seen, the cereals all appear to be members of the grass family, from which they differ merely in having very abundant and large grains. Biologists usually explain this as due to artificial selection through the ages. This means that they would not be what they are, apart from breeding by man.

Theosophists, who are convinced of the fact that

each species of plant has its group soul, naturally interpret this relation to man as a special occult link, similar to the tie that exists between man and his domestic animals.

There is a further tradition among some schools of theosophists. They believe that man, at a certain stage in his evolution, was helped by some high initiates coming from the planet Venus. They have reason to suppose such helpers exist, and the recent idea of interplanetary travel makes it seem that advanced beings could reach the earth.

Moreover, it is claimed that the said beings not only gave moral or social guidance to mankind, but brought with them wheat grains, to supply a better cereal, also bees to produce honey and fertilize flowers, and also ants. Rye, they think, has been produced by man, in imitation of wheat, by selective breeding. Oats and Barley, they believe, are hybrids raised by crossing with earthly grasses.[1]

We may add that maize is probably the most modified of the cereals by human intervention.

Myth and Magic

From the materialistic point of view, bread is the staff of life because it keeps the body performing its activities in a satisfactory manner. From a spiritual point of view it symbolizes the permanence of the immortal part of man, it is, in symbolism, the spiritual and celestial food of Swedenborg, the manna from heaven. This was understood in pre-Christian times.

The Greeks had a goddess of corn called

[1] A.E. Powell: *The Solar System*, London, 1930.

Demeter, better known (when taken over by the Romans) by the Latin name of Ceres. According to some, Demeter simply means the barley-goddess.

Now on two occasions Ceres, as we will call her, had withdrawn from Olympus, the residence of the gods; in other words she had taken such action that the cereal crops had begun to fail everywhere. On the one occasion that was caused by the loss of her daughter Proserpina (Persephone *Gk.*) who had been carried down into the earth by Pluto the King of the Underworld to become his wife. Afterwards Proserpina was allowed to return to earth for six or (some say) nine months.

On the other occasion the withdrawal of Ceres from heaven was due to her being disgraced by her brother Neptune, whereupon she retired into a cave, and was eventually only enticed out by the gods assembling outside the cave and entertaining themselves in a noisy manner, whereupon Ceres, being filled with curiosity, came out to see what was happening and was persuaded to stay out. The same story is told, in Japanese mythology, of the sun-goddess Amaterasu and her brother, with several identical details.

The Eleusinian Mysteries

The teaching of these two myths is obvious. The physical property of the corn was the maintenance of the health of the body. The occult property of the corn was the upholding of the welfare of the spiritual life of man. But how was this to be accomplished? The myth was to be put into practice by means of the mysteries. The most famous of the mysteries of this goddess were the

Eleusinia among the Cretans and Greeks and the *Thesmophoria* among the Greeks. These two were closely connected.

The Eleusinian mysteries were reckoned the greatest of the religious initiations of the classical world. They were strictly secret, but all the most famous men of antiquity belonged thereto, except Socrates. They were supposed to be founded by Cadmus (1550 B.C.), Erechtheus (1399 B.C.) or Eumolpus (1356 B.C.) and were only abolished by the Emperor Theodosius I (a.d. 389) after they had spread to Rome.

Already in the Eleusinian mysteries the cult of Ceres, the goddess of corn, was associated with that of Bacchus, the god of wine. This foreshadows the use of bread and wine in the chief Christian sacrament, which is dealt with more fully in our chapter on Herbs in Religion.[1]

Bean King and Queen

We now come to the pulses, such as beans, peas and lentils. In the ancient Roman festival of the *Lemuria* black beans were cast upon graves. Beans were also burnt. It was thought that this, and other associated practices, such as beating of drums and uttering of magical words, would prevent the ghosts of the dead from troubling the living. On the other hand, legumes seem to have been consumed in a reverent manner at funerals, from which it appears that their occult properties were such as link the living and the dead.

Pythagoras is said to have forbidden his followers to use beans. Some say this means he forbade them

[1] See page 65ff.

to take public offices, as such were elected by votes
taken in the form of beans. Aristotle says beans
signify lasciviousness; thus the prohibition of using
beans might mean chastity.

It has also been suggested that unruly conduct in
general is signified by peas and beans, because of
the wild and unruly growth of their shoots.

On Twelfth Night in mediaeval France and
England, young people were chosen to play the part
of a king and queen by hiding two beans in a large
cake which was cut up amongst the company. The
youth and maiden who were served with the beans
were given certain privileges.

In a somewhat similar way the Lord of Misrule
was appointed at Hallowe'en to serve at the King's
Court until Candlemas. He was a sort of court-fool
and was called Abbot of Unreason in Scotland.
The custom was abolished in 1555, but traces of
similar foolery have been preserved in our
Universities.

Carling Sunday

This is better known as Passion Sunday. It was also
called Care Sunday. On this day there was a
custom of eating peas, called carlings. They were
steeped, then fried with butter, then given away.
We have seen that beans were associated with
funerals and on Passion Sunday was celebrated, by
anticipation,[1] the funeral of Christ.

Beans and peas represent the souls of the dead.
Beans were hallowed by the Roman clergy on this
day, being brought to the altar. This, also, was

---

[1] Because Lent, consisting of forty days, represents the forty
hours between crucifixion and resurrection.

practised by the Greek Church. Sown seed must be moist. Except it be buried it will not grow (*John* xii, 24-25). The deepest humility is symbolized by burial. For this reason (in the East) some yogis originally practised the art of being buried alive.

Apple Cult

Apples have been said to have followed acorns as the chief food for primitive man. But apart from their nutritive value it may be seen, from numerous ancient beliefs and superstitions, that apples have an occult reference to love.

On the Eve of Christmas or Twelfth Night an apple-cult was still in vogue in Britain and some other European countries until the early part of the present century. The object was to ensure a good crop. It included visits to the orchard, perambulations of the trees, recitations referring to fertility, beating the trees with sticks or shooting at them, making loud noises, wassailing (drinking health to the trees in cider), dipping branches in cider, offering toast, cheese and roasted apples, pouring cider on the roots. Sometimes a boy climbed a tree and personified the tree spirit.

Sometimes the spirit was personified by a tit, wren or robin, which in ancient times was sacrificed. Hence the old custom of hunting the wren and the nursery rhyme, *"Who killed cock-robin?"*. In some places the fiddle was played, after which the fiddler would place his head on the knees of each maiden present and pronounce the name of her future husband.

Divination by Apples

Some time before Michaelmas, maidens gathered

crab-apples and cut into them the initials of their suitors, leaving the fruit to dry. On Michaelmas day they examined them and the initials seeming most perfect were considered to represent the most likely husbands.

On the day of Saint Simon and Jude, apples were pared, the parings thrown down and supposed to represent the initials of the future husband.

Another way of divination, practised at Hallowe'en, was catching apples in the mouth, suspended on a string or floating in a bucket. If a maiden, combing her hair, and holding an apple in her mouth, were to look in a mirror, she might, so it was believed, catch a glance of her future husband. A couple, sharing an apple, were likely to marry.

All this is quite in harmony with classical mythology. The golden apples of the Hesperides, for instance, were given by Juno to Jupiter on the day of their wedding.

At the wedding of Peleus and Thetis, when all the gods and goddesses were present, except the goddess of discord, who had not been invited, the latter threw into their midst a golden apple bearing the inscription; *"For the fairest"*. (Juno, Minerva and Venus) between whom the judgment was to be given by a mortal. Paris was chosen to be the judge, and he awarded it to Venus, thus precipitating the Trojan War.

In another story the beautiful but athletic princess Atalanta, to free herself from the importunities of her many suitors, says she will marry the first one of them that can outrun her in a race. Not one was successful until Hippomanes competed. He was no better a runner than the others, but he had been provided by Venus with

three golden apples, which he threw down during
the race. Distracted by this, Atalanta allowed
Hippomanes to win and he thus became her
husband.

Other Fruit Ceremonies

There were many other ceremonies connected with
fruits, some of which are witnesses to special or
general occult properties. Naturally a very general
connection with fruits was with fertility. This is
logically associated with feasts of the dead, since
death requires new life for replacement, hence
fertility. All Souls' day (Nov. 2nd) is celebrated for
all the dead, not only by Christians, but by
Buddhists and Druids. Its eve, celebrated for all
Saints by Christians, was the feast of Pomona,
goddess of fruit, amongst the pagan Romans.
Hallowe'en (All Souls' Eve) has been called the
Christian equivalent of this, and – more vulgarly –
Nutcracker Night, because of certain divinatory
practices with nuts, especially the hazel. It was the
Keltic Samhain, also a feast among the pagan
Franks and Germans.

Among the most important tree cults were those
of the fig, sacred to Pan, the vine, sacred to Bacchus
(to be dealt with later), the olive, sacred to Minerva
(see also later) and the pomegranate, sacred to
Juno.

Harvest festivals are numerous. One of the oldest
is the Jewish Feast of Tabernacles. In this occurs
the carrying of four kinds of plants: the *lulac* or tall
palm branch, the *esrog* or citron, the *hadassim* or
myrtle and the *arovous* or willow. The first three
signify the beauty of God's gifts, the last is to teach
humility.

Japanese Tea Ceremony

Tea was introduced into Japan from the mainland of Asia in the eighth century, but did not become popular until the thirteenth. Shortly after, the influence of Zen Buddhism began to make itself felt in the realm of tea-drinking, and a Buddhist monk brought over from China a complete set of utensils for the proper preparation and serving of tea.

As is well known, Zen claims to teach a direct approach to hidden human abilities. Hence there was supposed to be a proper mode of serving tea, as there was in many other arts! Besides this it was said that tea was favourable to meditation, as it maintained awareness. The tea-room was decorated with the utmost simplicity and the movements of the ritual were extremely harmonious.

Tea was also consumed in large quantities in Tibetan monasteries.

Other Tisanes

Tea was introduced into Europe in the sixteenth century and soon became popular. It is made by treating the dried leaves of the tea-bush (*Thea*) with boiling water, and such preparations are called *tisanes*. They also include coffee from the kernels (so-called beans) of the coffee-plant (*Coffea*), roasted and ground, cocoa from the powdered seeds of *Theobroma*, and maté tea from the dried leaves of a species of *Ilex*, a plant of the holly genus, widely used in South America.

CHAPTER THREE

HERBS IN HEALING

From historical and archaeological studies we now have extensive lists of plants used by the ancients in the art of healing. Some of these are still included in the modern pharmacopoeia, whilst others have been eliminated. In spite of the introduction of depth-psychology into modern medicine, drugs are now expected to have a chemical action on the body. Even those affecting the mind are assumed to work by chemical action on cells of the brain.

Pomegranate was used by the ancient Babylonians and Egyptians, but is now regarded as useless. The Babylonians used turmeric, now regarded nothing more than a colouring agent. Spikenard, a most important drug of the Hebrews and Hindus, is now reduced to a mere adulterating material found in some samples of valerian. Mistletoe, to which the Druids ascribed almost miraculous powers of healing, is no longer mentioned in our books on pharmacognosy.

Occult Properties

It appears that the ancients were aware of occult properties of herbs, which they believed had effects on the invisible aspects of man, which are thought to be purely imaginary by the materialistic science of the present day.

Only a few clairvoyants have dared to talk about this sort of thing in recent years. In 1906 an old gentleman called himself Charubel published a book[1] dealing with the cure of disease by sympathy with herbs and stones on what he called the soul plane.

Later Dr Rudolf Steiner, founder of the Anthroposophical Society, introduced medicines based on his investigations of spiritual science, and these included mistletoe. Steiner believed spiritual elements worked through physical substances, so that his methods were not antagonistic to, but complementary to, modern medicine.

The casting out of devils, well known from the New Testament, was believed to be possible, among the Babylonians, Egyptians and Hindus by the act of injection of an enema or clyster.[2] Most of the modes of administration, known to pharmacists today, were of ancient origin.

Ayur-veda, the Hindu System

The four Vedas are the most important of the Hindu scriptures and the *Ayur-veda* is the medical supplement to one of them, said to have been written by Dhanwantari, the physician of the gods. It treats the subject from an exceedingly broad point of view, for *Ayu* means simply life.[3] It alleges

[1] *Psychology of Botany*, Leigh, 1906, giving psychic impressions of thirty-nine plants, three metals and eleven precious stones, with symbols appropriate to each.

[2] C.J.S. Thompson: *The Mystery and Arts of the Apothecary*, London, 1929.

[3] Our account is based on *Ayurveda or the Hindu System of Medicine* by B.V. Raman, edited and annotated by W.B. Crow, first published in *The Search Quarterly* IV, I 1934 and afterwards reprinted in Bangalore.

that health is the harmonious balance of the three important forces acting in the body and of its seven main tissues.

Disease is of three main kinds: physical, accidental and mental, but all three have a spiritual basis. Medicines also are of three kinds: (i) *mantras* (regulated sound vibrations) rites and offerings, plants and gems; (ii) articles applied with reason and (iii) freedom of the mind from injurious acts.

Herbs therefore only form a part of the treatment, yet many are utilized from the very abundant native flora of India. Many of these have been imported in Western medicine and used for their obvious physiological effects.

An example is *Rauwolfia*, a poisonous genus of the periwinkle family, long used in India as a purgative and antidote against snake and insect bites. This came into use in Europe as a tranquillizer some few years ago.

Nevertheless it is not for the physiological effects alone that the Ayurvedic drugs are used in India. According to Dr Raman[1] the following characteristics are taken into account: (i) the preponderant of the five *bhutas*[2] in the composition of the drug, (ii) its taste, (iii) its qualities, for example, liquid or solid, heavy or light, (iv) its potency or strength of action, (v) its after-effects, (vi) any special peculiarities. The Ayur-vedic practitioner also takes into account the season of

[1] Loc. cit.

[2] *bhuta* is translated element, but as Dr Raman points out, it is certainly not an element in the sense of chemistry; rather it resembles an element in the sense of the nature-philosophy or arcane science.

the year, the condition of the patient, his food and
every aspect of his environment.

Moxa

In China, from the earliest times, a system of
medicine has been in vogue which purports to cure
disease by inserting needles into various parts of the
body. This system is called *acupuncture*.

Special charts and models show exactly where
the needles should be applied. This system has
spread to Europe and has been much practised in
France. As it has nothing to do with herbs it is
outside the scope of this book.

However, the practitioners of acupuncture
sometimes use what is called *moxa*, and there are
separate practitioners of the latter. Moxa consists of
the use of small cones or cylinders of the powdered
leaves of mugwort (*Artemisia*), a composite plant
related to the chamomile, which are used as
counter-irritants.

These cones are placed on definite places on the
body, specified by moxa-charts, quite distinct from
acupuncture charts, set fire to by a taper or burning
joss-stick, raising a small blister into which the ash
may be rubbed. Even moxa has occasionally been
practised in Europe.

Doctrine of Signatures

In the Middle Ages in Europe a curious occult
property was ascribed to certain plants. It was
noted that certain parts of a plant might resemble
in form or colour some parts of the human body,
and it was believed that disease of the said organ

could be cured by the appication of the corresponding plant.

This was *the doctrine of signatures*, which stated that every plant was signed, as it were, with its own use, and it was only necessary to look for and understand the signature. In some plants this was easy.

The liverworts, for instance, were so named because the plant body often resemble a liver in shape. Consequently they were used for liver complaints. The lungwort, a plant allied to the borage and forget-me-not had leaves resembling the lungs and was used for the treatment of that organ.

The bladder-wort is a water-plant with submerged leaves upon which are born small bladders in which insects are caught. It was used in diseases of the urinary bladder. It is distantly related to the foxglove. The orchis, a Monocotyledon, receives its name from its underground tubers resembling the testes of the male body, therefore believed especially valuable for diseases of the male sex organs.

The birthwort, belonging to a somewhat isolated group of Dicotyledons, has enormous flowers, the corolla of which resembles the womb of the female body, consequently being used in female diseases, especially if connected with childbirth.

As regards colour, red sandalwood was used for diseases of the blood, as also were the petals of red roses. The yellow colour of saffron, from the stigmas of a monocotyledonous plant of the crocus type, was thought to resemble bile and consequently was used in the treatment of biliousness.

Herbalism

In the early Middle Ages physicians used many
herbs as their medicines, following the great
classical works of Hippocrates (460-377 B.C.) and
Galen[1] (*circa* A.D. 130-200), but about the time of
the Reformation, Paracelsus (1493-1541)
introduced many mineral drugs.

In England, the Royal College of Physicians
obtained letters patent in 1518 (during the reign of
Henry VIII 1491-1547) with powers somewhat
similar to those now possessed by the General
Medical Council. But about this time an Act of
Parliament was passed whereby anyone having a
knowledge of the healing properties of plants was
allowed to make use of such knowledge.

This Act was claimed as a charter by many
practitioners of folk-medicine, who had not studied
anatomy, physiology and the clinical subjects in a
medical school. They became known as herbalists.

The plants used at the beginning of the present
century were wild herbs (Dicotyledons) very few of
which were recognized as being of any use by the
regular medical profession. The following is the
list,[2] arranged according to families:

Loranthus   Family   (Loranthceae):   mistletoe
    (*Viscum*).
Dock Family (Polygonaceae): bistort (*Polygonum*).
Pink   Family   (Caryophyllaceae):   chickweed
    (*Stellaria*).

---

[1] Vegetable drugs are still called *galenicals* after Galen.
[2] From W.H. Webb (Ed.): *Standard Guide to Non-poisonous
Herbal Medicine*, Southport, 1916.

Rose Family (Rosaceae): agrimony (*Agrimonia*), meadowsweet (*Ulmaria*), wild raspberry (*Rubus*).

Bean and Pea Family (Leguminosae): broom (*Sarothamnus*).

Flax Family (Linaceae): mountain flax (*Linum*).

Lythrum Family (Lythraceae): purple loosestrife (*Lythrum*).

Carrot Family (Umbelliferae): sea holly (*Eryngium*), wild carrot (*Daucus*), wood sanicle (*Sanicula*).

Gentian Family (Gentianaceae): buck bean or bog bean (*Menyanthes*), centaury (*Erythraea*).

Borage Family (Boraginaceae): comfrey (*Symphytum*).

Dead Nettle Family (Labiatae): black horehound (*Ballota*), white horehound (*Marrubium*) ground-ivy (*Glechoma*), self-heal (*Prunella*), skull-cap (*Scutellaria*), wood betony (*Betonica*), wood sage (*Teucrium*), red sage (*Salvia*), water mint (*Mentha*), hyssop (*Hyssopus*).

Plantain Family (Plantaginaceae): plantain (*Plantago*).

Valerian Family (Valerianaceae): Valerian (*Valeriana*).

Sunflower Family (Compositae): burdock (*Arctium*), burmarigold (*Bidens*), coltsfoot (*Tussilago*), dandelion (*Taraxacum*), mugwort (*Artemesia*), ragwort (*Senecio*), yarrow (*Achillea*).

Herbalism spread to America with the pilgrim fathers and a rather distinctive set of plants came into use which included the following, of which the first two families are monocotyledonous:

Orchid Family (Orchidaceae): lady's slipper (*Cypripedium*).

Arum Family (Araceae): wake robin (Arum).

Myrtle Family (Myricaceae): bog myrtle (*Myrica*).

Birthwort Family (Aristolochiaceae): birthwort (*Aristolochia*), Canada snakeroot (*Asarum*).

Water Lily Family (Nymphaeaceaa): water-lily (*Nymphaea*).

Buttercup Family (Ranunculaceae): black snake root (*Cimicifuga*), golden seal (*Hydrastis*).

Barberry Family (Berberidaceae): barberry (*Berberis*).

Witch-hazel Family (Hamamelidaceae): witch-hazel (*Hamamelis*).

Wood-sorrel Family (Oxalidaceae): wood-sorrel (*Oxalis*).

Rue Family (Rutaceae): prickly ash (*Zanthoxylum*).

Wintergreen Family (Pyrolaceae): wintergreen (*Pyrola*).

Potato Family (Solanaceae): cayenne pepper (*Capsicum*).

Dead Nettle Family (Labiatae): pennyroyal (*Mentha*), water horehound (*Lycopus*).

Foxglove Family (Scrophulariaceae): balmony (*Chelone*).

Sunflower Family (Compositae): gravel root (*Empatorium*).

Lobelia Family (Lobeliaceae): *Lobelia*.

Many of these were taken over from the native Indian folk-medicine. *Lobelia* and *Capsicum* were the chief medicines of the Thomsonian system, so-called from Samuel Thomson (1769-1843) who introduced them. They were the cause of much controversy with the medical profession, who opposed the herbalists.

Homoeopathy

The system of medicine called *homoeopathy* was introduced by a medical man and has been practised by thousands of qualified physicians. But it differs from ordinary medicine, which its practitioners call *allopathy*.

The differences are as follows: (i) Every drug used in homoeopathy must have been tested on a healthy person, (ii) in such person the drug must produce exactly the symptoms of the disease it is used to cure, (iii) only one remedy is to be used at a time, (iv) the drug is used in its greatest possible dilution, in fact dilution is thought to activate the drug. Hence degrees of dilution are called *potencies*.

Homoeopathy was brought into existence by Samuel Hahnemann (1755-1843). Whilst translating Cullen's *Materia Medica* he noted a number of medicines, called *specifics*, which acted only in certain diseases. One of these was Peruvian bark from *Cinchona*, a South American plant of the madder family which was, at the time, becoming very popular in the treatment of malaria.

Being of an inquiring mind, Hahnemann tried this drug on himself and found he had developed symptoms similar to those of malaria, even in detail. He then, with the aid of friends, experimented with a wide range of drugs and found the same sort of thing.

Thus deadly nightshade (*Atropa Belladonna*) produces the symptoms of scarlet fever, poison ivy (*Rhus toxicodendron*) produces those of erysipelas, thorn-apple (*Datura stramonium*) those of asthma, colocynth (*Citrullus colocynthis*) those of colic, etc.

The drug is always used in small quantities,

dilluted with water or mixed with an inert powder, such as milk sugar (lactose).

Some of the early homoeopaths used such extreme dilutions that it is said that only a few molecules or none at all were available. This led to suggestions, such as we believe were put forward by the aforementioned Dr Rudolf Steiner, that occult or super-physical properties were involved. We understand some investigations along these lines have been made by the Anthroposophical Society.

CHAPTER FOUR

DRUGS AND POISONS

The cereals, as we have seen, whilst upholding the physical life of man, from the occult point of view are seen, in the ceremonies of Demeter or Ceres, as upholding the spiritual life. In the mysteries of Eleusis, we have remarked, the goddess was associated with Dionysus, the god called Bacchus by the Romans. The latter also had several festivals of his own in Athens.

Dionysus was the god of the vine, and hence of wine. From the occult point of view the wine is not merely an intoxicating liquor, but it can be used for spiritual purposes. At its lowest level this can be seen in the drinking bouts practised in the West Indies and among the Caribs of Central America, where, after drinking heavily, the drinkers fall down alongside graves, and afterwards relate messages that they receive from the dead.

At its highest level, intoxication with wine symbolizes divine ecstasy to the mystic. Although Islam forbids the use of wine, many of the Sufis, the mystics of this religion, wrote poems in praise of wine, using this symbolism.

Today certain people are claiming the use of new drugs in the expansion of consciousness. This mistaken idea was shared by the ancients in the use of wine. Consequently the cult of Bacchus in Rome degenerated into a series of orgies at one time. It was suppressed, but later reinstated, as it was realized that the proper use of wine in the mysteries had a profound occult significance. To this we will return later.

Fermented Liquors

On the skin of grapes a microscopic fungus called yeast (*Saccharomyces*) lives. When the grapes are pressed and the juice called *must* is obtained, the latter has the yeast cells within it and these cause, by a process of fermentation the conversion of the grape sugar into ethyl alchol (ethanol), the latter being the intoxicating principle.

Alcoholic liquors are also made from herbs containing other sugars or even starch. In the latter case the starch has to be converted to sugar by means of a living agent, and there are micro-organisms that do this. In a few cases human saliva has been used, for which purpose the vegetable matter is chewed! Spirits of course are prepared from fermented liquors which have been distilled, a process already known to the ancients.

Sugar in Nature

Apart from a few instances, such as mead made from honey,[1] the sugar available in nature comes from the vegetable kingdom. Noah was the first traditional cultivator of the vine after his egress from the ark.

Wine is therefore in use in the early stages of written history and is recorded from everywhere in Europe, although the vine will not grow in the colder countries. Wine was often imported. We

[1] Even honey is derived from nectar of flowers, although indirectly through the bee.

have already referred to cider, produced from apples. Perry, from pears, was made in a similar manner.

In Britain native plants were used at an early date, so a kind of wine was produced from sloe, gooseberry, blackberry, elderberry, rhubarb and even turnip. In the tropics other plants were used. The sugar-cane, probably a native of the East Indies, was also used in Africa, producing the wine called *massanga*.

A banana-wine was in vogue in East Africa. Palm-wine, derived from various palms, was produced in North and West Africa, India, Ceylon, the isles of the Pacific and South and Central America. Wine from the agave, called *pulque*, was widespread in Mexico and South America and in these regions even cacti were sometimes used.

Beer from Starch

As regards starch as a source of liquors, cereals were often used. Beer was brewed in ancient Egypt, and hence spread to Europe and the colder parts of Asia and finally to the rest of the world. It was made from *malt*, which is germinating barley grain.

Hops were not used in Egypt, but were added later for flavouring. Millet was used at a very early date for making a kind of beer in India, Tibet and Africa and is still used under the name of *pombé* in many parts of West Africa. Wheat was used for making *white beer* in Germany.

Rice was used in producing what was called *tuak* in Borneo and *saké* in China and Japan. Maize was the plant for producing *chicha* in Central and South America. Tapioca and yucca were materials for other drinks in the same regions. The last three examples were prepared by the aforementioned chewing.[1]

The vast number of different liquors that have received separate names depend on different flavours, partly due to the source, partly to special substances added or mixed, partly to the method of preparation. Flavour and mode of preparation will be referred to again in our chapter on magic.

It should be mentioned however that the making of the beverages was often associated with certain cults, not only were there exact rules in the preparation of the drinks, but also for celebrations, such as dacnes, songs and the like.

Tobacco

The tobacco plant (*Nicotiana tabacum*), a native of America and now cultivated in all warm countries, provides leaves which are slowly dried and slightly fermented. They are now used in all parts of the world (except by Sikhs, Parsis and a few others) in the following ways: (i) by chewing, (ii) as snuff, (iii) smoked in a pipe, (iv) as cigars, (v) as cigarettes.

These methods of indulging in the herb developed in the Old World rapidly, in spite of opposition, after the voyage of Columbus and other early explorers opened up the New World of America. The point of interest for us, however, is that not only were the native peoples of America, such as the Aztecs and Toltecs of Mexico and their redskin successors addicted to tobacco, but they made a cult of it.

[1] For many more details of these and other drugs see that classical work by L. Lewin: *Phantastica: Narcotic & Stimulating Drugs*, trans. London, 1964.

As pointed out by Lewin,[1] tobacco banishes vacancy of mind, boredom and the aggressive instincts, and produces a mild excitation, so that we can say that the occult property of tobacco, used correctly, is the production of the state of peace. Hence it is well known that North American Indians presented a *pipe of peace* to friendly people, and the same was smoked in an atmosphere of harmony in their assemblies. The same rite was even imported into Europe.

Opium

On cutting many plants a milky fluid called *latex* streams out, and afterwards hardens. It may be of different colours and quantities. Opium is the hardened white latex of the large capsules of the opium poppy (*Papaver somniferum*) which turns brown on keeping. This contains many alkaloids, the chief of which is morphine.

Whilst useful in medicine for the temporary relief of pain, the opium alkaloids are mostly dangerous drugs of addiction, the illegal spread of which it has been very difficult to suppress. The addicts use opium: (i) by consuming the dried latex by mouth, (ii) by smoking or (iii) by injecting morphine or one of its salts. We can hardly call this a cult, unless it be of sleep or death.

However, the ancients were well-aware of the effects of poppies and a female figure crowned with these flowers would represent Nox, the goddess of night, or a male similarly adorned would probably be Morpheus, the god of dreams, referring to the

[1] Loc. cit.

visions caused by the drug. He was said to be the
son of Simnus, the god of sleep.

Mescal

This drug, otherwise known as *peyotl*, consists of the
dried heads of the cactus *Anhalonium lewinii*. It
contains four alkaloids, the chief of which is called
mescalin and which appears to be peculiar to this
species.

Mescalin has very peculiar effects. It varies
somewhat with the individual, its chief effects are
visual, sometimes auditory, often with a disturb-
ance in the apparent sequence of time, and other
hallucinations whereby the taker believes himself to
be in another world.

The plant is indigenous to Mexico and parts of
the United States. The government of the latter
country has prohibited its use, but the natives have
made the eating of it into a cult, with assemblies
around a fire, music, singing, preparation of the
drug and other ritual actions.

Indian Hemp

Hemp plants are the source of an important fibre,
but Indian hemp (*Cannabis indica*) is a well-known
drug and is made into a beverage called *haschisch* or
hashish,[1] whilst the leaves and young shoots called
bhang and the resin obtained from the plants by
beating, called *charrus*, are smoked. The seeds are
also smoked. It was known in ancient times and in

[1] This name is often given to the plant itself; there are
distinct male and female plants, which is unusual in the
vegetable kingdom.

mediaeval times was much used in the Middle East, where attempts were made to prohibit it.

Hashish is chiefly famous for its use among the sect of the assassins, whose leader, called the Old Man of the Mountain, whose headquarters were on Mount Lebanon, used it to induce his followers to commit humerous political murders (1090-1272). Hence the word assassination is derived from the word hashish.

Some Other Vegetable Drugs

Cocaine is obtained from the shrub called coca (*Erythroxylum coca*) which was native to South America, but is now only known in cultivation in Peru and Bolivia, and places from which it has been exported.

The dried leaves of coca were chewed by the natives, mixed with lime or ash, and were said to impart powers of endurance, allaying fatigue, hunger and pain. The plant is distantly related to the geranium family.

In South America, among the natives of Ecuador, the woody climber *Banisteria caafie* yields *aya-huasca* from the stems, a beverage being prepared. It contains harmine, a substance related to mescalin. According to Lewin[1] its effects also resemble those of thorn-apple,[2] and like the latter it was used by sorcerers. The plant is again a distant relation of the geranium family.

In the Amazon valley grows another woody climber of the genus *Paullinia*, only very distantly

[1] Loc. cit.
[2] See page 32.

related to the preceding plant. It furnishes seeds which are scraped or ground to produce, with water, a paste (*pasta guarana*) from which a beverage is prepared. This is classed by Lewin[1] as an excitant. In the same region of the world a snuff called *parica* is prepared from the seeds of *Piptadenia peregrina*, a legume of the *Acacia* group.

Kava-kava is prepared as a beverage on New Guinea and many of the islands of Polynesia. It comes from the rootstock (rhizome) of a plant *Piper methysticum* of the pepper-family (Piperaceae). As the preparation involves chewing it was formerly thought alcoholic fermentation explained its properties, but Lewin proved that the excitant effects are due to a resin.

Among the Australian aborigines, *pituri* consisted of the powdered leaves of *Duboisia hopwoodii*, a plant of either the potato or foxglove families. Pituri was both chewed and smoked.

Throughout the warmer parts of Asia, especially on the islands from Madagascar to the Philippines, the nut of the betel palm (*Areca catechu*) is chewed.

Camphor: A Dangerous Excitant

In China, Japan and Formosa, camphor is produced from *Cinnamomum camphora*, a tree closely related to cinnamon. A volatile oil is distilled from parts of the plant, and the cyrstalline white solid is separated. It has been used in tinctures and pills for hundreds of years in Europe and it is a dangerous excitant, except in very small doses.

In Arabia an infusion called *khat* of the shoots of

[1] Loc. cit.

Catha edulis, a plant of the spindle-tree family (Celastraceae) is prepared. In the Yemen the shoots are chewed.

We must not forget to mention the *kola-nut*, native to the Sudan, from whence it has spread to many countries. The chewing of the nut is extremely popular in warm countries. It comes from *Cola acuminata*, a plant of the cocoa family (Sterculiaceae). There are many similar nuts, but they lack the excitant qualities of kola.

Finally we can include a drug called *kanna* or *channa* from succulents of the large genus *Mesembryanthemum* (Aizoaceae). This is used largely by the Hottentots of South Africa.

All the drugs mentioned in this section have an important effect on the social life of the various people using them. Although their physiological effects are now fairly well known, their psychological and sociological studies might reveal many curious phenomena worthy of engaging the interest of students of the occult.

Aphrodisiacs

A medicine stimulating the sexual instinct is called an *aphrodisiac* after the Greek goddess Aphrodite, called Venus by the Romans.

An aphrodisiac must not be confused with a love potion. The former is purely medical and is supposed to act on physiological phenomena; the latter is purely magical and is believed to act through occult forces. The former stimulates the sex force in general, the latter directs it to some particular individual.

Aphrodisiacs are the most unreliable of medicines; in modern medicine it might be said that they do not exist, or that many foods are aphrodisiacs. Certainly a diet that maintains one in health tends to uphold the sex instinct, as it does the instinctive life in general.

A poisonous drug like strychnine, used in small quantities to increase the tone of muscles, may possibly facilitate the performance of the sexual act, especially if, like yohimbine, it acts particularly on the pelvic musculature.

But it is now admitted, thanks to the investigations into the psychology of the unconscious, that sexual likes and dislikes are so influenced by the mind that the idea of direct action of drugs is ruled out. Even the materialist, today, believes the brain acts through or in harmony with the endorcrine glands: 'monkey-gland' treatment was tried out about thirty years ago and found to be unsatisfactory.

Some Aphrodisiacs of Repute

It may still be of interest, however, to record some of the aphrodisiacs of repute, remembering that even when successful, much depends on the correct dosage, and bearing in mind the opposing effects of small and large doses.

From the animal kingdom, musk and ambergris were used, also ants and certain beetles producing *cantharides*, a drug so often producing death.

Very many foods, such as garlic, onion, artichoke, cardoon, asparagus, beans, lentils, cabbage, carrots and celery were thought to possess aphrodisiac properties, and more especially many fruits and seeds, and anything of stimulating taste or odour, such as many spices, for instance, nutmeg, pepper, red pepper, turmeric, vanilla, capers, aniseed, caraway seed, horseradish, etc.

We have already referred to strychnine, a dangerous poison obtained from nux vomica, the seeds of *Strychnos nux-vomica*, a small tree of the *Buddleia* family (Loganiaceae) and to yohimbine, obtained from the bark of stems of *Pausinystalia yohimba*, a tree of the madder family (Rubiaceae).

A similar, if not identical, principle is obtained from the bark of the white quebracho (*Aspidosperma quebracho*), a plant of the periwinkle family (Apocynaceae). Less powerful are damiana and saw palmetto, which were commonly used together by herbalists in the form of tablets or pills.

Damiana consists of the leaves of *Turnera diffusa*, a herb of Central America, distantly related to the violet family (Violaceae). Saw palmetto or sabal, consists of the fruits of the palm *Serenoa repens*, having a nutty, vanilla-like colour.

Poisonous Plants

The upas-tree (*Antiaris*) of Java, a member of the mulberry family, is reputed to be the most poisonous of plants. Vapours from this plant were supposed to kill off vegetable and animal life for miles around. This story is based on the fact that the tree grows in certain low valleys where volcanic vapours do destroy life, but not vapour from the tree. It furnished, nevertheless, an arrow-poison for the natives.

The same applied to three species of *Euphorbia* in Africa, one species of the same genus in Brazil, whilst in Guiana a species of *Strychnos* (different from the one yielding strychnine) and still another in Java, are also used for the same purpose.

A very poisonous latex comes from the

manchineel (*Hippomane*) of the Euphorbia family in
Central America and the West Indies.

An arrow poison used by the Zulus comes from
the genus *Acokantheria* of the periwinkle family.

Many genera of the Euphorbia family are
poisonous, for example, *Croton, Codiaeum,
Toxicodendrum*. Some members of the pea and bean
family, such as *Crotalaria* (sunn-hemp) and
Physostigma (ordeal bean of Calabar) are poisonous.
The cashew family (Anacardiaceae) includes the
poison ivy, the poison oak and the poison sumach,
all members of the genus *Rhus*.

Queen-mother of Poisons

The monkshook *Aconitum* has been called the queen-
mother of poisons. It is a native of Britain and
cultivated for its flowers. Another poisonous genus
of the same family (Ranunculaceae) *Helleborus*
includes the hellebore and Christmas rose, whilst
Veratrum of the monocotyledonous Lily family
(Liliaceae) is the white hellebore.

Many other poisonous plants have been
mentioned and will be mentioned later. They are
found in most families. But in some families, such
as the carrot (Umbelliferae) and potato
(Solanaceae) branches, they are particularly
abundant.

CHAPTER FIVE

HERBS IN ALCHEMY

Elsewhere we have stated our belief that alchemy was an antique and mediaeval science concerned with three main problems: (i) the making of gold, (ii) the finding of the elixir of life, and (iii) the art of producing living things from the non-living.

Before the days of alchemical laboratories, however, preserved on Babylonian tablets, the oldest of which goes back to the second millenium B.C., is the Gilgamesh Epic, in the latter part of which the great hero Gilgamesh, after the death of his friend Enkido, goes on a long and complicated journey in search of the herb of immortality.

Eventually, after great difficulties, Gilgamesh reaches the paradise of Uta-Napishtim, the Babylonian Noah, who has, after the flood, been given immortality by the gods. Gilgamesh is told, however, that it is impossible for a mortal to attain immortality by earthly things, but is permitted to share a great secret, namely that at the bottom of the sea in a certain place is a prickly plant and any old person eating the same regains his youth.

With further difficulties Gilgamesh obtains this plant, and makes for home. On the way back he stops to bathe and lays the plant aside. On emerging from the water he sees the plant is carried away by a serpent and all his efforts have been in vain.

Elixir of Life

Whilst the Hindus and Buddhists looked for regeneration in yogic practices affecting the vegetative soul of man, some of the mediaeval recipes for the *elixir of life* contain herbs, but usually only as accessories, the main ingredients being something unknown.

The idea that there was a single substance that could cure all diseases, however, was very prevalent in the Middle Ages. Such a substance was called a panacea. In *The Thousand and One Nights* there is a reference to the apple of Samarcand, which is a cure for every disorder. This may be founded on the existence of some fruit used in healing in early days.

Other Fruits Called Apples

Besides our ordinary apple there are other fruits called apples. The custard-apple, the sugar-apple and the alligator-apple are species of *Anona*, related to the cherimoyer, and some are edible. The love-apple is the tomato (*Lycopersicum*).

The elephant-apple or wood-apple (*Feronia*) is also edible, and so is the rose-apple or Malay apple (*Eugenia*). The may-apple (*Pododphyllum*) belongs to a drug-yielding plant. The pine-apple (*Ananas*) helps in the digestion of protein.

The star-apple (*Chrysophyllum*) is edible. The thorn-apple (*Datura*) is thorny and poisonous, although it has been used in medicine in minute doses.

Blood of Prometheus

Another elixir of life was the *Promethean unguent*, made from a herb from which some of the blood of

Prometheus had fallen. In mythology the witch Medea gave some of it to her lover Jason, to preserve him from burns and wounds.

In Sir Walter Scott's *Pirate*, the dulse of Guiodin, a sea-weed, will cure every disease except the black death.

In China the ginseng, a species of *Aralia*, was often regarded as a panacea. Elephant's foot, a species of *Hydrocotyle*, a plant of the carrot family, is another. In the thirties a newspaper report recorded the death of a Chinaman who had thrived on this herb, dying at an age well over two hundred years.

Palingenesy

Certain writers of the middle of the seventeenth century claimed to know of a peculiar substance, which unfortunately cannot now be identified, whereby a plant could be apparently resuscitated from its ashes.

A plant was burnt, its ashes carefully collected and treated in a certain manner with the special substance. A blue powder resulted. This was placed in a suitable vessel and gently heated.

Under the influence of the heat the powder assumed the ghost-like form of the plant from which the ashes had been taken. On withdrawal of the heat the apparition disappeared, but could be reproduced by further heating. Similar experiments were recorded for animals and even human beings.[1]

Spontaneous Generation

The ancients believed that plants and animals,

[1] For further details see Lewis Spence: *An Encyclopaedia of Occultism*, London, 1920, article 'Paligenesy'.

besides being born from other plants and animals by seeds, egg and other ways, might arise from non-living substances.

Even Aristotle, who was so accurate in many observations on living things, thought vertebrates such as eels, frogs and serpents might be born from mud.

The modern view,[1] that living things (including micro-organisms) always arise from other living things of the same or similar species was not fully established until the work of L. Pasteur (1822-1895). It was not surprising, therefore, that the alchemists thought it possible to produce living things, including human beings,[2] in an artificial manner.

[1] For some account of the history of the controversy see W.B. Crow: 'Spontaneous Generation', *The Search*, 1933, or, for a shorter account, the same author's *A Sypnosis of Biology*, Bristol, 1960 and 2nd edition, 1964, p. 2.

[2] For a brief account of this see W.B. Crow: *A History of Magic, Witchcraft and Occultism*, London, 1968, p. 209.

CHAPTER SIX

HERBS IN ASTROLOGY

Properly understood, astrology is a study of some of the rhythms[1] of nature and of man. Whilst it includes far more than the materialist can imagine, we will first point out that, in the history of the earth, plant and animal life were quite different at different epochs.

From the study of fossils we learn that in the oldest rocks (pre-Cambrian and Cambrian) there are remains of algae and bacteria, in the next (Ordovician) very simple fish-like vertebrates appear but land-plants are doubtful.

In the next period (Silurian) land plants not much above the moss level appear, some land scorpions and many true fishes, in the next (Devonian) still more fishes and plants like giant club-mosses and horsetails, in the next (Carboniferous) fern-like plants, insects, spiders and amphibians among animals, in the next (Permian) reptiles and cone-plants flourish. These epochs constitute the Palaeozoic.

Now comes the long age of reptiles (Mesozoic) and it was not until the third division of this (Cretaceous) that the flowering plants become abundant. In the following (Tertiary) era the various families of the same evolved.

[1] W.B. Crow: 'Biological Rhythms the basis for Scientific Astrology', *Proteus*, I, Jan. 1931 and 'Further Biological Rhythms', *Proteus*, 4, Oct. 1931.

Seasons

While in the tropics seasonal changes are less noticeable, in the temperate zone they affect both animal and plant life profoundly. There are times for seed to be set, times for germination, budding, shedding of leaves, flowering, fruiting and dispersal of seeds. Different plants flower at different times. To illustrate from the British Flora:

January: speedwell (*Veronica*), winter aconite (*Eranthis*);

February: lesser celandine (*Ficaria*), dog's mercury (*Mercurialis*);

March: marsh marigold (*Caltha*), wood anemone (*Anemone*);

April: bluebell (*Scilla*), ladies' smock (*Cardamine*);

May: wood sanicle (*Sanicula*), hawthorn or may (*Crataegus*);

June: dog-rose (*Rosa*), wild thyme (*Thymus*);

July: bindweed (*Convolvulus*), Traveller's Joy (*Clematis*);

August: ivy (*Hedera*);

September: Meadow saffron (*Colchicum*);

October: *Sternbergia*, allied to preceding (Mediterranean);

November: *Leycesteria* (Himalayan) of the elder affinity;

December: Christmas rose (*Helleborus*).

A similar table could be constructed for germination, budding, ripening of fruit and other phenomena.

Plants and the Moon

It has long been believed that the growth of
vegetation varies with the phases of the moon.[1] In
1929 L. Kolisko[2] published results of some
experiments which had been carried out during
several years. These showed that in wheat plants,
which were the subject of the experiments, there is
an increase of growth with the waxing moon, but
there is also a yearly cycle, growth decreasing on
the whole towards the winter months. Both factors
must be taken into account.

In fact, in December the usual increase towards
the time of the new moon does not occur, and there
is a remarkable acceleration of growth before the
Easter full moon. During the fortnight before the
latter,   additional   growth   more   than
counterbalances the usual effects of the waning
moon.

Similar results were soon after obtained with
maize, and since that time other important results
of research have been published by workers, mostly
among the anthroposophists.

The Floral Clock

The fact that flowers open and close at different
hours of the day and night led Linnaeus (1707-
1778) to suggest the so-called floral clock, whereby
one could tell the time, very roughly, from
observing which flowers are open or closed.

The difficulties are: (i) flowers open and close at

[1] For some account of lunar rhythms in plants, animals and
the human subject, see W.B. Crow, 'Lunar Rhythms', *Proteus*, 5,
Jan. 1932.

[2] 'Der Mond und das Pflanzenwachstum', *Gäa Sophia*, IV,
1929.

different times at different latitudes; (ii) the flowers most useful for constructing such a clock are not all flourishing at the same time of the year. Nevertheless, attempts have been made to plant the clock in public gardens.

The original list was constructed by Linnaeus for Upsala, 60°N a second by Kerner[1] for Innsbruck 47°. A list giving English names was published by Brewer.[2]

Herbs of the Planets
The flowers of the floral clock cannot correspond with the planetary hours, since the latter depend, not only on the 24-hour cycle, but also on the cycle of the week.

As each day of the week corresponds with a planet we might expect a 7-day cycle. We suggest the clue to this might be found in the 28-day lunar cycle divided by the four elements: fire, earth, air and water, which do play a part in astrology.

But to consider now the traditional rulership of herbs according to the seven planets we must remind any readers who are not acquainted with astrology that the sun and moon, called luminaries, are counted with the seven planets.

Solar Herbs
The sun rules Sunday and passes through the zodiac in one year. Consequently the solar herbs are mostly of annual growth and symbolized in old herbals by the sun's symbol ·.

---

[1] Both these lists are published in Kerner, *The Natural History of Plants*, trans. Oliver, 2nd vol., London, 1902.

[2] *Dictionary of Phrase and Fable*, London, 1895.

Alternatively these herbs would show one of the signatures of the sun, namely, (i) a golden or orange colour, like saffron or the orange;[1] (ii) an orbicular shape; (iii) a large size; (iv) a radiating shape, e.g. sunflower; (v) an aromatic odour; (vi) an action on the heart, i.e. as cordials, from *cor* the heart, ruled by the sun, like cinnamon; (vii) a tendency to turn towards the sun, for example, sunflower and heliotrope.

Moon Herbs

The moon (symbol ☽) rules Monday and passes through the zodiac in twenty-eight days. Its herbs have: (i) soft juicy leaves; (ii) often live in freshwater; (iii) the flowers and fruits are white or pale yellow; (iv) the fruits are large; (v) also watery and tasteless, like the melon, pumpkin and gourd; (vi) they are believed to show a marked monthly periodicity; (vii) they show lunar signatures, e.g. the shape of the gibbous phase of the moon in the fruits of honesty (*Lunaria*), the crescentic leaves of moonwort (*Botrychium lunaria*) and the crescentic gemma-cup of *Lunularia*.

Mars for Biennials

The planet Mars rules Tuesday. It passes through the zodiac in, very roughtly, two years, consequently its sign ♂ was formerly used for biennials.[2] Its plants (i) possess thorns, spines or prickles, e.g. hawthorn, sloe, bramble, thistles; (ii)

---

[1] Orange also shows signature (ii) and (iii).
[2] Now used in biology for the male sex, being shield and spear, whilst the sign of Venus ♀ (looking glass) indicates the female.

live in dry places, even deserts, for example, cacti; (iii) have acrid pungent or stimulating properties like raspberry or red pepper; (v) show a red colour, like the red rose with its red thorns, or (vi) show a conical root called a tap-root (which also may be red, as in carrot or beet).

The planet Mercury (Symbol ☿) rules Wednesday, and passes through the zodiac in three months. Its herbs (i) have fine or highly divided leaves or stems, owing to the airy nature of this planet, e.g. grasses; (ii) have a subtle odour, for example, aniseed; (iii) have a medicinal effect on tongue, lungs and nervous system; and (iv) are important as food, notably the cereals.

Herbaceous Perennials

The planet Jupiter rules Thursday and passes through the zodiac in roughly twelve years. Its symbol ♃ indicated herbaceous perennials, which often live about twelve years. Its herbs (i) show the signature of the cross, e.g. Cruciferae, as the god Jupiter ruled over all the four quarters of the globe; (ii) they are large and conspicuous, for example, fig, olive and grape; (iii) they are edible and nutritious, typified by the acorn and beech-nut; (iv) they have a pleasant odour, as indicated by the mulberry, cloves, nutmeg and marjoram.

The planet Venus (Symbol ♀) rules Friday and passes through the zodiac in nine months. Its herbs (i) have beautiful flowers, white or pink,[1] as some roses; (ii) a pleasant smell, as rose and lily of the valley; (iii) smooth, green foliage and fruits,

---

[1] The pink colour is the feminine counterpart of red, as Mars (red) is the lover of Venus.

sometimes with a blushing tinge of pink or red, for example, apple.

Woody Perennials

The planet Saturn rules Saturday and completes its course through the zodiac in thirty years. Its symbol ♄ is used for woody perennials, the majority of which often live thiry years or thereabouts, although some trees live much longer.

The plants of Saturn (i) show annual rings, as Saturn is the god of time; (ii) have grey or dull foliage or bark; (iii) their flowers are scaly or insignificant; (iv) they are woody, even if not shrubs or trees, for example, tortoise-plant (*Testudinaria*) of the yam family (v) they have dull green foliage; (vi) unpleasant taste, and smell, such as valerian; and (vii) are often poisonous, namely, hellebore of the buttercup family, hemlock and many plants of the carrot family and deadly nightshade and many plants of the potato family.

Plants of the Zodiac

The author has proposed, following ancient tradition, a zodiacal classification of the vegetable kingdom.[1] Pisces, the fishes, obviously rule the algae, which includes the pond-scums and seaweeds.

Aries, the ram, signifying the pioneer, rules the lichens, plants that resemble seaweed in form, yet are pioneers on land, preparing the way for other vegetation. Taurus, the bull, signifying the earth,

[1] Also of animals and minerals, see 'The Astrological Correspondences of Animals, Herbs and Jewels', *Mysteries of the Ancients*, 2, London, 1942.

rules the fungi which mostly grow near (mushroom) or under (truffle) the ground.

Gemini, the twins, an airy sign, rules the mosses, many of which grow as epiphytes, i.e. on trees in the air. Cancer, the crab, a watery sign, rules the ferns, horse-tails and club-mosses, the sexual stage of which lives in water.

Leo, the lion, a fiery sign, rules the cone-plants, cycads, pines and firs. The cone is a signature of fire and the sun which rules this sign.

Virgo, the virgin, an earth sign, dedicated to Ceres the earth-mother, naturally rules cereals, grasses and sedges.

Libra, the balance, ruled by Venus, rules the most beautiful flowering plants such as iris, lilies and orchids.

Scorpio, the scorpion, rules aroids and palms; these plants have a phallic signature and Scorpio rules sex.

Sagittarius, the centaur, rules the great forest trees bearing catkins, such as the oak, beech and elm, for his sign rules forests.

Capricorn, the goat, rules the plants having flowers with separate petals.

Aquarius, the water-pourer, rules the plants having flowers with united petals.

CHAPTER SEVEN

HERBS IN MAGIC

Both in ancient Egyptian and Hindu creation legends, the first object to make its appearance was a golden egg, or sometimes it was a lotus or water-lily, floating on the primaeval waters. It bursts open, revealing the supreme God.

Iamblicus (d. A.D. 333), Neoplatonic philosopher, explained the round leaves and spherical fruit of the lotus as symbolic of intellect, its coming up from the mud as the supremacy of mind over matter, the deity as seated on the flower, on the surface of the water, as intellectual sovereignty.

Everywhere in ancient Egypt the sculptures, even the heads of columns, display the lotus. It was regarded as sacred in India, Tibet and China. There were three forms of lotus in Egypt: the white *Nymphaea lotus* with toothed leaves and round buds, the blue *Nymphaea caerulea*, and the red or rose *Nelembium speciosum*. The last named is mentioned by Herodotus (5th century B.C.) but no longer grows in the Nile.

The blue lotus, which has a pleasant smell, was certainly the most sacred. The dead and the living are shown smelling it and presumably performing some sort of spiritualist cult.

Druids and Mistletoe

The Druids were the priests of the Keltic peoples of Gaul, Great Britain and Ireland. They were supreme lawgivers. Kings and chiefs held office under their authority. They also acted as physicians and were teachers of all branches of learning.

Whether they used large stone temples, like Stonehenge, is debated. But it is certain they had a vegetation cult in which the oak was sacred, but the mistletoe growing on the oak still more so.

The mistletoe is planted on a tree by a bird. The latter, it has been suggested, was the symbol of the Holy Ghost, the mistletoe was the Messiah, and the oak the tree of Jesse. The Druids cut off branches of mistletoe with a golden sickle and distributed them to their congregation. That gold alone may touch the sacred plant reminds one of the Christian Eucharist.[1]

The Druids paid attention to all sorts of other plants and had an alphabet in which each letter was represented by a tree or shrub.[2] The bards were under the supervision of Druids. They were not poets in the modern sense, in that what they recited were magical compositions.

Rosicrucians and the Rose

The Rosicrucians first became known to the public when certain anonymous publications appeared in Germany in 1614, 1615 and 1616. They traced their society to a certain Christian Rosenkreutz who was supposed to be born in the fourteenth or fifteenth century and lived one hundred and six years. His tomb was supposed to have been discovered shortly before the appearance of the publications.

Thereafter, many writers claimed to disclose

[1] W.B. Crow: 'Druids and the Mistletoe Sacrament', *Mysteries of the Ancients*, 14, London, 1944.

[2] See page 83.

facts of interest about the secret fraternity. They
were opponents of the Papacy, they were advocates
of a world reformation in science, they possessed
secrets of alchemy and healing and later were said
to have connections with Freemasonry.

The puzzling question about the Rosicrucians is
how the rose on the cross came to be their chief
symbol. It is (i) certainly connected with the name
of their alleged founder; it is (ii) possibly connected
with the coat of arms of the anti-papal Luther, and
the Lutheran minister Andreae, who is said to have
written one of the manifestoes; (iii) the rose from
ancient times was a symbol of secrecy and (iv) the
rose, as the queen of flowers may symbolize the
activation of the vegetative life of man, being
combined with the cross, as the lotus did when
activated by Kundalini in yoga.

Love Philtres

As we have previously indicated, aphrodisiacs and
love philtres are quite different. Aphrodisiacs are
physiological in action, love philtres act through
occult forces and properties. Aphrodisiacs, it is
supposed, merely increased sexual libido, love
philtres direct it at some particular person.

Love philtres were often complex mixtures.
There is always a simple or complex magical
ceremonial in making a love philtre act, often
involving blood or bodily excretions. The
constituents of a love philtre were often of animal
origin, involving whole animals (for example,
spiders), hair, feathers, animal tissues and parts,
with or without herbs.

The philtre in the love affair of Tristan and Isolde

was said to be wholly herbal. The only really pleasant love philtre we have noted is that of Oberon (in Shakespeare's *A Midsummer Night's Dream*) which he gives to Titania to make her dote upon the first thing she sees when she wakes from sleep, the object being to recover one of his pages that Titania had taken from him.

Love-in-Idleness

The plant used was called love-in-idleness and has been identified with the pansy (*Viola tricolor*). Others, often used in real life included fern rhizome, black helebore, cinquefoil, cummin seed, verbena, marjoram, tobacco, mandrake, valerian and white bryony, which are mostly dangerous or nauseating.

For making potions for love and fertility no plant was more highly regarded than the mandrake (*Mandragora*) a plant of the potato family. For the root of this plant was said to resemble the whole male human body, except for the head, the place of which was taken by the overground green shoot.

The difficulty was that when pulled from the earth the mandrake screamed and anyone who heard it died. To obviate this a dog was tied to the shoot and dog-food placed, visible to the dog, but out of reach. The operator rode away quickly, the dog struggled and eventually pulled up the root, sacrificing its life in its heroic efforts. Naturally, mandrake was very expensive.

Herbs in Divination

Hundreds of different methods of divination are

recognized, named according to the objects used. Divination by means of plants is called *botanomancy*. It is largely used for revealing the future of one's love life, e.g. prospective husband or bride and the character of the same.

One form of this divination consists of a competition in which parties of boys and girls look for a certain arrangement of ash leaves. The first from each party to find it are supposed to get married.

With nuts, divination is made by naming each nut after a person, and then heating on a fire. Whether a nut burns rapidly or slowly, or jumps suddenly, have different meanings.

Bachelors Buttons

Bachelors' buttons was a name given to flowers of a common genus (*Lychnis*) of the pink family, also sometimes to other flowers. They were so-called because they were said to be carried about by bachelors in the hope that if they flourished the carrier would be successful in love.

Sometimes onions were named or marked and set beside the chimney and the first to sprout indicated the future marriage partner. An ivy-leaf named on New Year's Eve, inspected on Twelfth night, will show signs of the person named. Flowers were made into garlands, used in various divinatory games.

The readings from tea-leaves and coffee grounds has been widely practised. For this form of divination certain cups, marked out on the inside into areas of various significance, have been produced.

Plants used in Witchcraft

Witches[1] supplied love potions and poisons and by what we now term the power of suggestion caused untold suffering to innocent people, especially children. Witches also attended meetings, 'the witches' sabbaths' or more correctly *sabbats*.

To prepare herself for a sabbat, the witch stripped herself naked and rubbed an ointment all over her body. The ointment was called *flying ointment*, and was of several different kinds. It nearly always contained fat from the body of a murdered unbaptised infant, mixed in many cases with an extract of aconite, leaves of poplar, hemlock, water hemlock, sweet flag, cowbane, cinquefoil, thornapple and deadly nightshade. Some of these are dangerous poisons.

Certain medical authorities believe that the active principles of such plants might be absorbed through the skin and would induce a state of trance, during which the subject might imagine she would be transported through the air in a sort of dream, and there engage in a number of perverted and criminal acts. However, actual meetings of witches certainly did occur.

Antidotes to Enchantments

People protected themselves against witchcraft by holy water, consecrated salt, by candles hallowed at Candlemas and leaves blessed on Palm Sunday. Protection was also given by cinquefoil, whitethorn, vervain, St John's wort, olive, palm, orchis and

[1] For a further account of the witch cult see W.B. Crow: *A History of Magic, Witchcraft and Occultism*, London, 1968.

other herbs. Witches were kept away by the fumes of frankincense and myrrh.

The horse-shoe over a door-way is a relic of protection against witches. The five-pointed star was formerly used.

Trees as Oracles

At times, trees act as oracles. Moses heard the instructions of God from the burning bush (*Ex.* iii, 2-22). There are other references to speaking trees in the Old Testament. The prophetess Deborah gave pronouncement under a palm-tree near Bethel. David was given the signal for attacking the Philistines from a pear or mulberry-tree.

The great oracle of Apollo at Delphi was founded at the place where the nymph Daphne was supposed to have been changed into a laurel. The famous place, however, was originally a cleft in the earth, from which fumes issued, dedicated to the Earth-goddess. The pythoness, under the influence of the fumes, pronounced the oracle.

Dodona, in the Epirote mountains, depended on a great oak, the message being obtained from the sound of weapons and instruments suspended from the branches. These were interpreted by doves, as the priestesses of the cult were called. There were many other oracles in Greece, Rome and ancient Egypt. The Zoroastrians possessed one at the Holy Plane Tree at Armavira in the Caucasus, the pre-Islamic Arabs at the Sacred Palm at Nejran in the Yemen.

CHAPTER EIGHT

HERBS IN RELIGION

The gods and goddesses of Greece were supposed to live on Mount Olympus. They owed their immortality to the fact that they fed on *ambrosia* whilst their drink was *nectar*. Although some may think ambrosia refers to some powerful hallucinatory drug, secretly used in the Eleusinian mysteries, we are convinced it was nothing but bread.

We do know that the Epopteia in these mysteries corresponds with the Christian Mass, except that bread was believed to be the body of the goddess Demeter and wine the blood of Dionysus. The Roman author Cicero (106-43 B.C.) jeered at the belief that bread could be transformed into a deity, but he did not understand the mysteries.

In Egypt, barley represented the god Osiris, and the germinating grain was planted in the figure of the god. The same was seen in the so-called gardens of Adonis. Both gods belong to a class of deities that die and are resurrected to immortal life. This dogma is represented in all religions. The tulasi, a plant of the genus *Ocymum*, of the basil family, used as a condiment, was very sacred in India.

Among the Teutonic peoples apples were the food of the gods and mead was their drink. Among the Aztecs of Mexico maize and blood were used.

Nectar
To the Greek and Romans, red wine was the

nectar. Wine was also used by the Druids, Jews, Egyptians, Chinese and Tibetans.

The Hindus said *soma* was the drink of the gods, but it was well known to be nothing more than the juice of *Asclepias*, a plant of the periwinkle family, in everyday life. The Zoroastrians used *haoma*, which was the juice of *Ephedra*, a plant distantly related to the cone-bearers.

The Christian Mysteries

In the Catholic Mass, wine is transubstantiated into the blood of Christ and bread, in the form of wafers, into His body. In the Gospels (*John* XV, 1) Jesus describes Himself as the true vine. At the Last Supper He said the bread was His body, the wine was His blood (*Matt.* xxvi, 26, 27; *Mark* xiv, 22, 24; *Luke* xxii, 19, 20; *Cor.* xi, 24, 25). His words are repeated by the priest at Mass.

The bread is placed on a dish called a *paten*, and the wine in a cup called the *chalice*. Water is added to the wine, following an old Jewish custom. The wine was said to represent the divine nature of Christ and the water His human nature.

However the Armenians do not mingle water with the wine, as they do not believe in the two natures of Christ, which is why they are termed *monophysites*. In some Oriental Catholic rites the wine is simply unfermented grape-juice.[1] In most, however, the wine is fermented, as in the Western (Roman) rites. The bread is unleavened in the

[1] E.S. Drower: *Water into Wine*, London, 1956. This is the standard work on the usage of bread and wine in near Eastern rites both Christian and non-Christian. Lady Drower says the Mandaens also use unfermented wine.

Roman, Maronite and Armenian rites. Elsewhere
in the East it is leavened.[1]

The bread used by all Christians is made from
pure wheaten flour and was baked in olden times,
as it still is in some Eastern rites, by the clergy
themselves, or by the virgin girls. Prayers were said
during the baking.

The wafer or *host*, as it is called, is round and
stamped with some sacred device, usually the cross
or the letters IHS, the latter being an abbreviation
of the Greek *ichthys*, meaning a fish, the symbol of
Christ.[2]

Complicated Patterns

The breads used by the Oriental Catholics are
larger than ours and are marked out in complicated
patterns. A square piece in the centre, called *the
Holy Lamb* (the lamb being another symbol of
Christ) is cut out. This alone is consecrated, the rest
is used for the *antidoron*, i.e. bread distributed after
the Mass.

The bread is cut with the *lonche*, a small spear or
lance, and stabbed with the point of the same, to
commemorate the fact that when Jesus was on the
cross his side was pierced with a spear.

A piece of the consecrated bread is dropped into
the wine in both Eastern and Western rites. In the
East it is known as the pearl.[3]

---

[1] Thus we may count yeast, which is a fungus, as one of the
plants used in the Mysteries.

[2] Some early Christians, it is believed, actually had a fish
sacrament.

[3] For a legend connected with this see W.B. Crow: *Precious
Stones: their occult power and hidden significance*, London, 1968.

Nestorian Christians

A very curious custom is observed by the Nestorian Christians. On Maundy Thursday they make a mixture of flour, salt and powdered fragments of the consecrated sacramental bread, and at every Mass throughout the year they add some of the powdered sacramental bread. This mixture, called the *melka* is added by the priest when they bake their hosts.

Thus every new host, when consecrated, already contains tiny fragments of an old (consecrated) one, and the old ones contained traces of a still older and they say this sequence can be traced right back to the Last Supper. So their Hosts might be said to contain a homoeopathic dose of the bread used and consecrated by the Lord Himself!

Intinction in the East

Both in the West and in the East it is believed that Christ is really present both in the wine and the bread. As a consequence, communion may be in one or both species.

In the East it is given in both kinds, by *intinction* generally, that is, the sacred Host is moistened with the consecrated Wine and is often administered in a *labis* or spoon, although sometimes only the Wine is administered and sometimes the spoon is not used at all.

In the West the consecrated wafers are reserved in a vessel called a *ciborium* which resembles a chalice with the addition of a lid. This is kept in a veiled tabernacle or ark, either on the altar or at the side thereof. The object of reserving is so that the Sacrament can be carried to the dying, should the need arise.

Many of the Eastern Catholics do not reserve the

sacred Host, but consecrate it at any time required.
The Catholics of the Roman rite also use the
reserved Host for blessing the people. For this
purpose a *monstrance* is used, wherein the Host may
be seen by all, being sometimes carried in
procession through the streets.

Incense

In the West, incense is used at High Mass,
Benediction, Vespers and Funerals and in the East
at practically all public worship. The paschal
candle, which in recent Roman usage was blessed
and lighted on the eve of Easter, had five grains of
incense inserted into it, to represent the five wounds
of Christ. It burned for the forty days of Easter.

Incense is otherwise thrown on red-hot charcoal
in an incense-burner called a censer or thurible,
whilst the priest utters a special blessing. There are
special rules for using the censer, which is
suspended on chains.[1]

Sacred Oils

In the Christian Mysteries all the candles must be
composed of bees-wax and all the lamps must burn
olive oil. The olive is a tree widely cultivated in the
Mediterranean region. The edible fruit of the
cultivated variety is compressed to yield olive oil,
used in salads.

In the Catholic Church, both in the East and
West, olive oil and balsams are consecrated on
Maunday Thursday, the day which commemorates
the Last Supper. The consecrated oils are treated
with great respect, second only to the reverance

[1] The nature of incense is dealt with in chapter 12.

paid to the Body and Blood of our Lord. There are
three kinds of oils, according to consecration and
use, but all three are olive oil, with or without
balsam. They are as follows:

1. *Oil of Catechumens:* this takes its name from its
use in baptism, since those preparing for baptism
were called catechumens. The same oil is used for
blessing the font, the consecration of altars and
temples, the ordination of priests and the
coronation of kings and queens.

2. *Oil of the Sick:* called *prayer-oil* in the East,
used in the sacrament of healing and, curiously
enough in the blessing, or so-called baptism, of
bells.

3. *Chrism:* this alone being a mixture of olive oil
and balsams,[1] it is used in blessing the font, in the
sacrament or mystery of unction or chrism, in the
consecration of bishops and formerly of kings, in the
consecration of chalice and paten, and, very
remarkably, in the blessing of bells.

Linen

A plant that plays an important part in the
Mysteries is flax (*Linum*). For flax yields linen, one
of the most remarkable of textiles.

Egyptian mummies were swathed in linen. Linen
cloths are used in Catholic sacraments, presumably
because Jesus was buried in Egyptian fashion. We
need only mention the three altar cloths that cover
the altar, the *corporal* on which chalice and paten are
placed, the *pall* placed at times over the chalice, the
purificator used for wiping the inside of the chalice,

---

[1] For further details of balsams, see chapter 12.

after the same has been washed out with ordinary wine and water.

In the East a single linen cloth, the *poteriokalumma*, serves the functions of the pall and sometimes also the purificator. The Easterns also have a cloth which is placed over the paten; it is called the *diskokalluma*, also a fine cloth called the *aer* to cover both.

Some of the moderns, as in Russia, do not always use linen. The Easterns also have a ritual object, called the *asterisk* to prevent the veils touching the Host on the paten. Each of these objects has a symbolic significance. Thus the asterisk, which is star-shaped, represents the star of Bethlehem.

CHAPTER NINE

SYMBOLISM OF HERBS

An *emblem* differs from a symbol in that it is purely arbitrary. It is an entirely conscious thing, whereas a *symbol* refers to the unconscious, and may be only known to the initiated, or to others by revelation. Both may be learnt. It is somewhat difficult to distinguish between emblems and symbols. Some of the plants ascribed to certain places may have been symbolic, but their lore has now been lost. Others have been added in arbitrary fashion.

Among the best known emblems of countries are the rose for England, the leek for Wales, the thistle for Scotland, the shamrock for Ireland, the lily (*fleur-de-lis*) for France, the pomegranate for Spain, the linden for Prussia, the mignonette for Saxony, the violet for Greece, the maple for Canada. In the United States each state has its floral emblem.

Symbols of Gods

Herbs and other plants were very generally connected with gods, playing a part in myth, sacrifice or some form of ritual.

In ancient Egypt the acacia was sacred to Osiris, the absinthe to Isis, the sycamore to Hathor and Nuit, the peach to Harpocrates. Among the Babylonians the cedar was dedicated to Ea, among the Persians the cypress to Mithras.

In India the lotus formed the throne of Brahma, the pipul and the banyan and all members of the fig genus were consecrated to Vishnu, the wood-apple or bel-tree to Siva. Buddhists that Buddha attained enlightenment under the bodhi-tree.

Among the Chinese, Lao-tse was symbolized by the plum, Confucius by the bamboo and Buddha by the pine. They were called the three friends. The three star gods are connected with the peach.

Greek and Roman Plant Symbolism
It is among the Greeks and Romans that we have the most frequent references to plant symbolism. The vine for Bacchus and wheat for Ceres have already been mentioned. Bacchus also took ivy and fig. The latter was also given to Pan.

Saturn was also said to take the fig, but probably the bramble (Rubus) and the dragon-plant (*Dracunculus*) are more correct. Jupiter as king of the gods had the palm.

The dogwood was assigned to Mars, the laurel to Apollo, the apple to Venus, the mulberry to Mercury, the dittany (a plant of the dead-nettle family) to Diana.

The olive belonged to Minerva, the sugar-cane to Cupid, the poplar to Hercules, the cypress to Pluto, the mint to Proserpina, the knapweed to Chiron, the aconite to Cerberus, the quince to Juno, the heliotrope to Sol, the tamarisk to Luna, the plane to Helen, the golden apples (oranges?) to the Hesperides, the beech to the Golden Fleece, the narcissus to the Fates.

Symbols of Saints
In Christian symbolism even God is represented by some herbal symbols. Shamrock represents the Holy Trinity. Bread and wine represent the Saviour. The dove flower and the seven-petalled

columbine were regarded particularly as plants dedicated to the Holy Ghost. The symbol of the dove is well known for the Holy Ghost and His seven gifts are symbolized by the seven petals.

Many flowers were assigned to the Virgin Mary. In a mediaeval litany the chaplet of Mary consists of rose, violet, marguerite, marjoram and rosemary, each representing a particular virtue. St Mary is usually symbolized by the white lily, seen in pictures of the Annunciation. The rose is then assigned to St Mary Magdalene.

Certain plants are named after saints in folk-lore. Lady's smock (*Cardamine pratensis*) is only one of about a dozen different plants probably named after Our Lady. St John's wort (*Hypericum*, several species), St Barnaby's Thistle (*Centaurea solstitialis*), and Herb Christopher (*Actaea spicata*) are three examples of herbs named after saints.

The handsome plant called Crown Imperial (*Fritilaria imperialis*) is said to have received its name from St Edward the Confessor, King of England (1002-1066).

In art, numerous symbols are used to distinguish different saints, and among these one will find a number of plants used in the symbolism.

Symbols of Virtue

Under this heading we propose to list a few examples of virtues, vices and abstract ideas.

Among Christians the rose represents charity, the olive peace, the myrtle compassion, the mignonette mildness, the myrrh continence, the lotus chastity, the orange-blossom innocence.

Of course vice was symbolized too. The plant called basil, the name of which was thought to connect with the deadly reptile, the basilisk, was supposed to show anger, the stinging nettle portrayed gluttony, the hellebore calumny, the bramble envy, the poppy sloth and the cedar pride.

Death was symbolized by the yew, which was grown in burial grounds. Resurrection was represented by foliage of box. Immortality was well shown by the amaranth. Because of its small size and enormous production the mustard-seed represented omnipotence (*Matt*. xiii, 31; *Mark* iv, 31 and *Luke* xiii, 19).

Victory was represented by the palm, and was often shown in connection with martyrs.

Heraldic Herbs and Trees

In coats of arms every conceivable kind of symbol is shown. Naturally plants are numerous. They often have their usual symbolism, in addition to something connected with the life of a particular individual or family.

Of trees the oak, olive and palm are favourites. Others are the almond, apple, pear, cherry and walnut. The pine is the commonest of the cone plants.

The herbs are usually those with notable flowers, such as rose, lily, hyacinth and amaranth. The shamrock is, of course, very significant. The pomegranate is a favourite fruit. Some small herbs like darnel and house-leek occur for particular reasons.

Heraldry not only concerns itself with grants of coats-of-arms, but also deals with the conferring of honours. One of the most peculiar of all honours is the golden rose, conferred by the Pope.

With this honour goes an actual model in gold,

originally a single flower, later a small branch system with several flowers, richly ornamented with precious stones and red enamel to symbolize the Passion and perfumed with ambergris and musk. A special blessing was devised for it on the fourth Sunday in Lent.

The rose is usually received only by queens. King Henry VIII however received it before he fell out with the Pope. More recent awards were in 1861 to the Queen of Spain and 1862 to the Empress of the French.

CHAPTER TEN

MYTHICAL PLANTS

The materialistic science of the last century gave us a picture of the universe in the form of globes rotating and revolving in space and time. Its language was mathematical.

The spiritual science of ancient and mediaeval times, the truth of which is now being vindicated by the findings of depth psychology, represents the universe, or rather the spiritual Whole, as a temple, a tree or a mount, or more especially an integrated combination of all three. And of course this was represented in mythological language.

The tree grew on the mount of the gods, Olympus of the Greeks, whereon was their home, which was also their temple. The tree was situated "in the midst of paradise" (*Gen.* ii, 9) but in many myths it was taken for granted its branches reached to the confines of the universe.

The Egyptians, Hebrews, Phoenicians, Persians, Druids, Norsemen, Hindus, Chinese, Japanese, the Maories of New Zealand, the Aztecs of Mexico, the Mayas of Yucatan and the Incas of Peru, all had this tree.

Kabalistic Tree of Life

Among the Hebrews the tree developed into the philosophical kabalistic diagram of the *tree of life*, on which hung the ten sephiroth (*sing.* sephira). Each was represented by a pomegranate of a particular colour.

There is, of course, an extensive literature on the Kabalah, with which some readers will be familiar.

Norse World-tree
The Norse version of this myth is also very definite, as it has been recounted in the Prose or Younger *Edda*. The world-tree is a gigantic ash, situated in the middle of a mountain on which the gods meet in council. Its branches reach "above heaven".

Three great roots pass out, widely separated. They are described briefly thus: (i) goes to Niflheim, a sort of cold, damp, dark hell, where lives the wolf Fenris, whilst underneath the root is a fountain of spring called Hvergelmir and nearby the serpent Nidhug for ever gnaws the root; (ii) goes to the land of the frost-giants, Jotunnheim, with its chief city Utgard; beneath this root is the well of wisdom, guarded by the giant Mimir; (iii) goes to the land of the gods and under this root is the sacred fountain of Urd, attended by the three Norns or Fates.

On the branches of the tree four harts gnaw the shoots. They represent the four winds or four elements. An eagle perches on the topmost branch, and between the eyes of the eagle is a hawk.[1] A squirrel climbs up and down the tree, carrying messages causing conflict between the eagle and the aforementioned snake.

This world-tree of the Norsemen is called

---

[1] A bird on the tree is mentioned in some of the myths of other cultures, for example, see page 59 (bird planting mistletoe).

Yggdrasil, which means the gallows of Ygg or Odin, the King of the gods, who was supposed to have been hanged on it for nine days.

Bodhi-tree

Among the Buddhists a tree was associated with each buddha, as a plant was associated with each god fo the Greeks and Romans. In art the best known was the pippala, peepul or bo-tree (*Ficus religiosa*), under which Gautama, the historical buddha, attained enlightenment.

This tree, and the related *F. indica* and *F. benghalensis*, are about the most bulky plants in existence, as their branches continue outward growth much more extensively than do those of other trees, being supported by down-growing roots looking like trunks. So a single plant mimics a whole woodland. It is not surprising that this is the Buddhist version of the world-tree.

Three Seeds

When Adam and Eve were expelled from the Garden of Eden, according to legend, they took with them, (or according to another account, sent) their third son, Seth, to the gates of the garden to obtain three seeds of the tree of life.

From these seeds were raised trees which furnished (i) wood for the rod of Moses; (ii) the branch that was used to sweeten the waters of Marah; (iii) the wood used in the building of Solomon's temple; (iv) the wood for constructing the bench on which the Sibyls sat when they prophesied the coming of Christ; (v) the wood from which the Cross of Christ itself was made.

The legend is represented in a picture over the altar of a church in Leyden, Holland.

Archetypal Man

It is interesting to note that the Kabalists often show the archetypal man on their tree of life. Also that the cross of Christ is called a tree (*Acts* v, 30; *Acts* x, 39; *Galatians* iii, 13; *I Peter* ii, 24).

Zoroaster was fabled to have been suspended on a tree and was called the *splendid light* of this tree. As sacrificed gods, both Adonis of Syria and Attis of Phrygia were connected with vegetation.

Osiris of Egypt, a vegetation god, was killed by entombment in a box which eventually lodged in an acacia or tamarisk tree. Krishna, supreme incarnation of Vishnu in Indian mythology, was killed by an arrow which nailed him to a tree.

We have already mentioned Odin. Many other instances connect the incarnate sacrificed god with the tree.

Tree Spirits

Most students of the occult know the difference between *elementaries* and *elementals*. The former are spooks or shades of the dead wherein the immortal spirits is delayed, for a time, before passing on to a higher realms. They include ordinary graveyard ghosts and those that occasionally haunt old houses.

Elementals on the contrary, are nature spirits. They are of a lower order than angels. They are not immortal, like the latter, but can be made so, according to belief, by cohabiting with human beings.

There are six main classes[1]: *gnomes*, the spirits of earth, *undines* of water, *sylphs* of air, *salamanders* of fire; *dryads* of vegetation and *fauns* of animal life. Here we can only deal with the dryads.

In classical times each tree was supposed to be inhabited by, or in some way connected with, one of these spirits or nymphs, who died with the tree itself. These were called *hamadryads*. Offerings of milk, oil and honey were frequently made to them by country folk, and witches would occasionally sacrifice a goat.

The dryads also included those who were group spirits of herbs, as distinct from trees, also probably the *oreades* who presided over mountains, and *napaeae* over hills and dales.

Metamorphoses

Human beings, in classical mythology, were sometimes changed into animals or plants. This no doubt refers to psychological change and the particular living thing into which the victim was metamorphosed corresponds with the occult property involved.

In Ovid's *Metamorphoses* there are many of these changes. Of those involving vegetable life, the nymph Daphne was changed into a laurel to escape the advances of Phoebus, Syrinx into reeds because of the lust of Pan. The youth Narcissus, to avoid the opposite sex, especially the talkative nymph Echo, ws changed into the flower of that name.

[1] For some account of the classes not dealt with in this book see pages 110 and 111 in W.B. Crow's *A History of Magic, Witchcraft and Occultism*, Lodon, 1968.

Clytie, a nymph deserted by the sun-god, was changed into a sunflower, which turns its head to the sun. Adonis, the lover of Venus, when wounded by a boar, was changed into a myrrh tree for committing incest with her own father.

However, there were supposed to be antidotes for such transformations. For example, in the *Odyssey* the hero uses moly, a plant of the onion genus (*Allium*) to restore to human form his companions turned into swine by Circe. Garlic, another plant of the same genus, was in later times used against vampires.

Barnacle Geese

Metamorphosis in myth foreshadowed the discovery of the same sort of thing actually taking place in nature, for example, the transformation of the tadpole into the frog.

There were several imaginary metamorphoses of this kind, namely the belief, which was maintained until at least the seventeenth century, that (according to some) the pine or fir type trees, near the North-West coasts of Scotland and Ireland, grew barnacles and from out of the barnacles came barnacle geese.

There is a real, although superficial, resemblance between the appendages of a barnacle and the feathers of a bird.[1] To the student of occultism there is no reason why an occult affinity should not exist between a tree, a barnacle and a goose, in spite of the fact that there is no physical metamorphosis

[1] A full account is given in E. Heron-Allen's *Barnacles in Nature and Myth*, London, 1928.

and that they belong to totally different types of structure and therefore different realms of nature.

Druidical Tree Alphabet

We have seen that in mythology, to each god there was dedicated one or more special plants. In Keltic mythology there was a special list of gods with their corresponding trees. This accounts for such myths as *the battle of the trees*. The trees were almost to be regarded as totems of clans.

The original Gaelic alphabet was also in correspondence with this tree list. It consisted of seventeen letters. Later H was added (the Uath or whitethorn). It ran: BLNFS(H)DTCMGPRAOUEI, each letter being represented by the name of a tree.

Today the alphabet follows a more usual sequence and goes something like, this: Ailm, Beite, Coll, Dur, Eagh, Fearn, Gath, Huath, Togh, Luis, Muin, Nuin, Oir, Peith, Ruis, Suie, Teine, Ur.

The corresponding trees are: Elm, Birch, Hazel, Oak, Aspen, ALDER, Ivy, Whitethorn, Yew, Rowan or Quicken, Vine, Ash, Spindle-tree, Pine, Elder, Willow, Furze, Heath.

CHAPTER ELEVEN

BARKS AND WOODS

In some of the barks used in medicine their healing powers are indicated by an aromatic odour as in the West Indian canella, the cinnamon of Ceylon, the cascarilla of the Bahama Islands, the cassia of Indo-China, the sassafras and slippery elm of the U.S.A., and several others. These mostly come from different families, but cinnamon and cassia are both related to the laurel.

No Aroma

The barks possessing no aroma also include representatives of different families. They include those of pomegranate, spinkle-tree, black haw, wild cherry, cascara sagrada, cinchona and witch-hazel. Black haw is not related to hawthorn, but ·to the wayfaring tree. Cinchona, from S. America is the source of quinine.

Witch-hazel is in a family of its own (Hamamelidaceae) in the rose order. It was so called because its twigs were frequently used as divining rods. It is the shape, however, that facilitates divining, not the wood. The material of which a divining rod is composed may be anything, mineral, vegetable or animal, as the faculty depends on unconscious human muscular movements.

The bark of birch, carried about by anyone, was said to protect against enchantments, whilst that of willow could prevent delusary visions. The bark of species of *Eucalyptus* is called iron-bark.

Woods

To go back to legend, an interesting question arises
as to wood which the cross of Christ was used for. A
common assertion favours aspen, because the leaves
of this tree are constantly trembling, with fear,
according to poets.

Another idea, mentioned by Sir John Mandeville
(d. 1372) in travel tales about 1371, was that the
cross was composed of four woods: the upright of
cypress; the cross-piece, palm; the base in the
ground, cedar; whilst the table of the inscription
was olive. He says the choice was made for
permanence.

Another idea was that the woods came from the
four corners of the earth. So the cross embodied
comprehensiveness both in time and space. A
different idea was that the cross was the mistletoe,
once a large tree, but punished by being reduced to
a parasitic shrub.

Many early writers, including Shakespeare,[1] say
that Judas Iscariot hanged himself on an elder. The
latter plant was grown in gardens to warn off
witches and warlocks. If caught, they might be
crowned with elder in disgrace.

The woods of hornbeams, of hazel and of willow
were all favourites for making the forked Y-shaped
baguette or divining road, as well as the previously
mentioned witch-hazel.

"Immortal Wood"

Some woods are very resistant. That of *Erythrina
glauca* of the pea family has been called "immortal
wood". It is durable, but not hard. Juniper wood is

[1] In *Love's Labour's Lost*.

immune from the attacks of worm-like creatures,
cedar from those of moths and spiders, whilst alder,
cedar, myrtle and yew are said to dispel fleas.

It must be remembered that wood, except in
herbaceous and very young woody plants, consists
of the living *sapwood* and the dead *heartwood*. The
latter, however, is as important to the plant as a
skeleton is to an animal. It is of course the
heartwood which is most resistant and used in
building and the manufacture of innumerable
articles. It is usually more deeply coloured than the
sap-wood.

The wood of Monocotyledons is totally different
from that of Dicotyledons. The wood of cone-
bearers is also different, lacking vessels, which are
regarded as more advanced elements.

Bamboos are grasses, being examples of
Monocotyledon stems used in building and the
manufacture of many objects. Like other grasses
they contain the mineral silica. Concretions of this
substance found in one species (*Bambusa
arundinacea*), known as *tabashir* are used in the East
in folk-medicine in many diseases.

Tobacco at one time was frequently flavoured
and the making of cigar boxes of cedar and juniper
wood was said to be because of the perfect blending
of their odours with that of the tobacco.

Medicinal Woods
Woods used in medicine include the aromatic
sassafras and sandal, the bitter wood quassia and
the coloured woods guaiacum, red sanders,
logwood and sappan.

Guaiacum has yellow sapwood and greenish-
brown heartwood and comes mainly from the West

Indies. Red sanders has pink sapwood and blood-red heartwood; it comes from South India and the Philippines.

Logwood, of which only the heartwood is used, is purple in colour, and comes from Central America. Sappan, of which heartwood is mostly used, has white sapwood and orange heartwood, and comes from India and the Malay Archipelago.

CHAPTER TWELVE

RESINS AND BALSAMS

A *mucilage* is obtained from the evaporation of a vegetable juice and is insoluble in alcohol or ether. As well known from their use as adhesives, mucilages form a sticky solution in water. A *gum*, in the narrow sense of the word, is used for a product of injury in a plant. These occur in nature, owing to the attacks of insects, injuries caused by the wind, etc. Both kinds are included as *gums* in the broad sense of the word. Gums in medicine have a use as mild demulcents and as a means of suspending drugs less soluble in water. They include gum Arabic, tragacanth, and carob gum. Other gums were used in magic. Cherry-gum, for instance, was used under the cryptic name of 'brain' in magical fumigations.

Kinos
Under this heading we include dried juices such as Malabar or East Indian kino from *Pterocarpus*, so-called red gum or Eucalytpus kino, and Bengal kino from *Butea*, of the pea family.

The only one used in magic, as far as our records go, was the dried juice of *Aloe* from the large leaves of this plant of the lily family. It was an ingredient in the magical fumigations of the sun, moon, and the two beneficent planets, Venus and Jupiter.

Gum-Resins
These are intermediate between gums and resins. They include galbanum, olibanium or

frankincense, myrrh, bdellium, ammoniacum, gamboge and asafoetida, all used in the medicine.

Asafoetida has an intense penetrating odour of the alliaceous type, and comes from a species of *Ferula* of the carrot family. It was used in magic and in Persia as a condiment. Even in the latter capacity it was thought to have remarkable occult qualities, as it was called 'the food of the gods'.

Myrrh, which comes from N.E. Asia and has an aromatic odour, was used in embalming and was therefore symbolic of death. In magic it was used in rites of the planet Saturn, the greater infortune. Bdellium, also from the East, was used in the rites of the planet Mars, the lesser infortune.

In addition to the *haoma*, which, we have already seen, was used in worship by the Parsis, they also make use of palm fronds and pomegranate twigs and formerly bundles of resinous twigs of barsam, which today are replaced by bundles of wires. The Parsis themselves seem unable to tell us exactly from what plant the twigs of the barsam are derived. But it seems likely that they belonged to the myrrh family (Burseraceae) and they may have been of the same genus as the myrrh (*Commiphora*).

Gifts of the Magi
The Magi, or wise men, who visited the infant Jesus offered gold, frankincense and myrrh. It is said that gold signifies His kingship, frankincense His priesthood and myrrh His death and resurrection.

In ancient times, gold and frankincense were offered in places as far apart as China and Peru to priest-kings. Myrrh was used for embalming in ancient Egypt to prepare the body for future resurrection.

It must be remembered that, in the Old World, the Jews and Christians practised mummification, as did the aboriginal inhabitants of the New World. Further, the body of Jesus, taken down from the cross, was bound up with spices by St Joseph of Arimathea and St Nicodemus 'as the manner of the Jews is to bury' (*John* xiv, 40).

These disciples used no less than one hundred pounds weight of myrrh and aloes. The last named was probably not the dried juice previously mentioned here and still used in medicine but a gum resin from the fragrant Indian eagle-tree *Aquilaria agallocha*, a Dicotyledon of doubtful affinity.

Resins

In the restricted sense, resins are plant products soluble in alcohol, ether and ethereal oils, but not in water. Sandarac, benzoin, dragon's blood and mastic are obtained simply by cutting. Colophony and Venetian turpentine are prepared by distilling away much of the liquid, when they remain as residues.

Mastic was used in magic for ceremonies related to the planet Mercury. Dragon's blood was also used under the cryptic designation of 'blood'. Mastic comes from a species of *Pistachia* of the cashew-family living in the Mediterranean region.

Dragon's blood is from the fruits of *Daemonorops*, a palm. It comes in clear, deep-red pieces several centimetres across but is often powdered. Another kind formerly came from the trunk of the dragon tree genus (*Dracaena*). It is in the form of smaller drops. These plants are tropical.

Incense in Worship

Benzoin is prepared by cutting stems of *Styrax*, the resin being formed as a result of wounding. The plants are native to, and cultivated in ,Sumutra and Siam. They are trees somewhat related to ebony. As benzoin and frankincense are the chief constituents of incense used in worship, we take this opportunity of adding a few remarks on this subject, some facts concerning which have already been given.[1]

In practically all religious worship, except among protestants and some Moslems, incense was used in the ritual. Among Hebrews it was prescribed by God (*Exod*. xxx, 1. 5), and there was a special altar of incense for daily use.

Although early Christians refused to offer incense to the deities of Rome, they were using it in their own worship, references of which are made in the *Apocalypse* of St John and the works of Origen. Materialistic writers, such as Maimonides, said incense was used in assemblies to counteract body odours, but although it may have this effect that is not its occult purpose, which is, as Leadbeater[2] remarks, fourfold: (i) symbolism of the ascent of prayer, (ii) spreading of divine influence, (iii) showing of respect and (iv) effecting purification.

Leadbeater goes on to say that the presence of incense, owing to what he calls its undulation rate, is favourable to spiritual vibrations, but hostile to almost all others. He goes on to mention its magnetized condition, as he calls it, effected by the

[1] See page 69.
[2] C.W. Leadbetter: *The Science of the Sacraments*. Madras, 1929.

priest, and to discuss the connection of the use of
incense with the inhabitants of unseen worlds.

The Thurible

Incense was used by the ancient Egyptians,
Hindus, Buddhists, Greeks and Romans. In
Lamaism the thurible or censer, in which incense is
burnt, closely resembles that usually carried in the
Western Catholic Church. There are, however, no
end of varities of thuribles, often made of very
precious material. A favourite shape was in the
form of some bird. This symbolized air, as did
incense itself, the idea being that all four elements
must be included in worship: holy water includes
salt and water, the salt representing earth, the
flames of the candles and charcoal represent fire,
whilst the incense vapour signifies air.

The formula for making a suitable incense to be
used by Moses is given in *Exod*. xxx, 34. It includes
galbanum and frankincense and several other
substances difficult to identify.

Oleo-Resins

The oleo-resins are intermediate between resins
and oils. They are balsams in the narrow sense of
the term. They are obtained by cutting, and in
some cases, such as balsam of Peru and Storax, are
caused by the wounding. The thick liquid which
oozes out on cutting gradually hardens to solid
form.

The balsams used in the making of chrism are
generally about six different kinds in the West and
thirty-six in the East. They must include at least
one constituent which is technically a balsam in the

broad sense of the term, which includes gum-resins, resins and oleo-resins.

The oleo-resins: balsam of Peru, balsam of Tolu and Canada balsam, come from the New World, so were not used by the early Christians. Storax, which comes from a genus (*Liquidambar*) of the witch-hazel family, is Turkish in origin and almost certainly was. It was also used in magic for ceremonies connected with the moon.

Oils

These include *fixed oils*, which are called fats if solid at ordinary temperatures, and the chemically different *essential oils* which contain volatile substances and are responsible for the fragrant odours of many flowers.

Camphor is obtained by distillation by oil from the wood of a plant from the cinnamon genus (*Cinnamomum*) of the laurel family. It was used in magic ceremonies of the moon. Clove oil is obtained from the flower buds of a plant (*Eugenia*) of the myrtle family. They were used in magical ceremonies connected with the planet Mercury.

Olive oil has already been dealt with. In the Old Testament (*Exod.* xxx, 23-24) the anointing oil was described as containing myrrh, cinnamon, calamus, cassia and olive.

In the New Testament, when St Mary Magdalene anointed Jesus and adverse criticism was made about this act, our Lord explained that she had anointed Him for burial. The ointment used was said to be of precious spikenard and was contained in an alabaster box.

If the translation be correct, spikenard is a plant

of the valerian family and the genus *Nardostachys*, the two species of which grow in the Himalayan region. The active principle is derived from the fragrant rhizomes (underground stems).

INDEX